Diving on the Edge

Also by Michael Bane

Over the Edge: A Regular Guy's Odyssey in Extreme Sports

White Boy Singing the Blues

The Encyclopedia of Rock

The Outlaws

Shifting Paradigms: Reshaping the Future of Industry (with Dave Garwood)

Diving on the Edge

A Guide for New Divers

Michael Bane

THE LYONS PRESS

Publisher's Note

Diving is inherently dangerous, and the advice and instructions in this book are not intended to take the place of a formal program of diving instruction offered by licensed instructors. No one should attempt any form of diving without successfully completing such a program.

Printed in the United States of America

Illustrations by Mitchell Heinze

Designed by Joel Friedlander, Marin Bookworks

10 9 8 7 6 5 4 3 2 1

Library of Congress Cataloging-in-Publication Data
Bane, Michael 1950–
      Diving on the edge: a guide for new divers / Michael Bane.
           p.   cm.
      Includes index.
      ISBN 1-55821-540-9
      1. Scuba diving.   2. Scuba diving—Psychological aspects.
  I. Title.
      GV838.672.B36 1998
      797.2'3—dc21   97-44823
                                        CIP

Thanks to Wings and Ani Stock; David and Susan Feeney; John and Shelley Orlowski; Hal Watts, Michael Menduno, Bill Belleville, Gary Gentile, and a few unnamed others who have put up with endless pestering questions over the years. Not only would this book not have been possible without their help, the last few years would have been a heck of a lot less fun.

For that reason, this book is dedicated to them.

Contents

v

1:

An

Intro

to the

Abyss

We are all, the fishman is telling me, *aquatic creatures at heart*. The fishman's name is Francisco "Pipin" Ferreras-Rodriguez, and he should know. On a single breath, he has descended to 440 feet into the warm seas off Baja. We swam together earlier in the day in the warm Caribbean. He drew a single breath on the surface then settled into the sand valleys between the coral gardens, seated in a lotus position. As he sat, eyes almost closed, the bright tropicals come to explore—first, the inquisitive, aggressive triggerfish, darting forward to touch the tips of his folded fingers; then the yellow and blue tangs; finally a fat parrot fish to swim around Pipin's fins.

I hovered nearby, an alien presence compared to the fishman's calm. To the fish, I suspect I was all noise and bubbles, my scuba regulator bleeding a steady stream of spent air up to the surface. But to me it was a moment of extraordinary calm, as if the fishman and I descended not just to another place, but also to another time, another dimension.

We seek water, Pipin is telling me, *because we come from water*.

Our beginnings, says the man who was once a simple spearfisherman in Cuba, are in some primordial ocean an unimaginable time in the past.

But somewhere, says Pipin, on some cellular level, we remember.

Is the fishman right?

How else to explain the attraction for those of us who live on the earth for the world under the seas?

Most of us, however, aren't fishmen (or fishwomen). For us, our contact with this amazing undersea realm will be with the mechanical assistance of scuba gear. Once an acronym—for "Self-Contained Underwater Breathing Apparatus"—the word *scuba* has entered our language as "a diver's equipment with compressed-air tanks for breathing under water." Even small towns have their own dive shops, and scuba lessons are available all over the world.

Learning to dive is a strange experience, both harder and easier than a person might imagine. Harder because, like the first astronauts, the potential diver must for the first time adapt to an artificial life-support system—a spacesuit, if you will. During the period of time the diver is under water, the basic functions of breathing, of rising and falling in a water column, and even of warmth—the necessities of survival—are provided by the scuba gear.

But diving is also easier than the novice might imagine. The underwater environment seems surprisingly natural—a return to a magical place.

The world of diving is huge, encompassing everything from the clear, warm sea dancing with rainbow-bright reef fish to a cold world where even the memory of light has faded to eternal darkness. It is the ethereal songs of the humpback whales, transmitted through the medium of water; the unblinking, unyielding stare of the tiger shark; the quick dart of an octopus. It is also the hidden realm of flooded caves, the haunting bones of great ships, the sense of a lost world.

Jacques Cousteau's miraculous Aqua-Lung has been around since the early 1940s. And since the television days of *Sea Hunt*, in the early 1960s, scuba has captured the media's attention. I remember reading the first of Ian Fleming's James Bond books, where the dashing British secret agent—licensed to kill, you know—braved endless undersea dangers with his wet suit, wits, and an occasional speargun. The movies, too, mined the undersea world, and the "frogmen" were the stars. Still, it has only been in the last decade that we've seen the tremendous boom in the number of recreational divers. Perhaps it's no wonder: As soon as we matinee kids were old enough, we headed for the closest dive shop.

This boom in diving has been a mixed blessing. While more people are able to see the underwater realm for themselves, the growing number of terrestrial visitors puts increasing pressure on a fragile ecosystem.

It's time we shift the way we view diving. In the past, the apparent goal of the dive industry was to certify as many people as possible, sell them equipment, and then move on to the next batch of prospective divers. Consequently, diving has ranked right up there with health club membership as a pastime that many try, but relatively few pursue.

This book approaches scuba as a lifelong sport, one for which obtaining a certification card is only the first step. It's not a "how-to-dive" book; there are already dozens of how-to books on diving. Nor is it an encyclopedia of the undersea world, or a catalog of nifty equipment you can buy.

Rather, *Diving on the Edge* is a book on how to start *thinking* about diving. As Americans—and I am certainly guilty of this myself—we tend to see a sport as a collection of gear to purchase; our instruction in the sport often includes little more than how to operate the equipment. Unfortunately, the corollary to this sort of thinking is the belief that after we've mastered the equipment, we've mastered the sport. And we get bored. *Diving on the Edge* offers the novice diver, or the potential diver, a clear path to follow for a lifetime of diving, and a rationale for following that path.

The book also operates from a strong ecological sensibility. No more riding turtles or rays. No more stepping on corals. Diver traffic has increased to a point that such ecological practices as maintaining neutral buoyancy (not sinking to the bottom and thus destroying whatever we land on) are no longer "advanced" skills; they are prerequisites. For reasons we don't yet understand, the great coral reefs are dying. Divers have a responsibility not to hasten their demise.

This book accepts and reinforces the fact that scuba is a risk sport: An understanding and acceptance of the risks of diving is a prerequisite for learning to dive. Statistics that "prove" diving is safer than bowling prove only the point made by Winston Churchill about "lies, damn lies, and statistics." If your bowling shoes fail, you are unlikely to end up in a decompression chamber—or dead.

The key to minimizing risks is information.

Finally, though, *Diving on the Edge* is founded on the principle that such information is useless unless it can be integrated into training and planning.

Scuba technology is poised on the edge of a spectacular leap. Rather than depending upon tanks of compressed air as the heart and soul of the underwater life-support system, divers in the very near future will be using rebreathers—computer-controlled devices that clean and recirculate the breathing mix. And in all probability, that breathing mix won't be air. Air has some definite disadvantages as we go deeper and deeper and our bodies absorb gaseous nitrogen. Instead, why not tailor the breathing mix to the depth? For shallow dives, we might increase the percentage of oxygen for a greater safety factor. At greater depths, we might decrease the percentage of oxygen and replace a portion of the nitrogen with helium—a combination called trimix—again, for safer dives.

Driven by such technological advances, the world of diving is changing. We need to be able to adapt to these changes—not as an exercise in mastering new equipment or reading manuals, but in order that we continue to be amazed and awed by the undersea world.

"We are," wrote the great climber Yvon Chouinard, "*Homo sapiens*, the tool users. We earn the name by developing tools to increase our leverage on the world around us, and with this increased technological leverage comes a growing sense of power. . . . So, in reaction, we set sail on the wide sea without motors in hopes of feeling the wind; we leave the Land Rover behind as we seek the desert to know the sun, searching for a remembered bright world. Paddling out again, we turn to ride the shorebreak landward, walking on the waves, the smell of wildflowers meeting us on the offshore breeze. In the process we find not what our tools can do for us but what we are capable of feeling without them, of knowing directly."

Of knowing directly. That is the secret of the fishman: to enter a different world neither as invader nor as tourist, but, as much as possible, on that world's terms.

2:
Toward an Underwater Environmental Ethic

Before discussing the underwater environment, I want to talk about the Heisenberg uncertainty principle. Originally conceived of by the German physicist Werner Karl Heisenberg before World War II, the uncertainty principle places an absolute limit on the accuracy of measurement. In layman's terms—and all you physicists out there hold your fire—the very act of observing a particle changes that particle.

If you bastardize it, you might say that what the uncertainty principle means is that when we look at something, we change it. Now, apply this to the underwater environment.

All divers became divers to spend time studying and enjoying the underwater environment. Do all those people have an effect on the world they're looking at? The answer, of course, is, yes, a tremendous one.

We change whatever areas we congregate in. It's the nature of our species; it's the way things work. Diving is no exception. But it's a little easier to see the changes created by the mobs of people at Yosemite, or the crowds around Old Faithful, or the hordes of Winnebagos at the Grand Canyon, than it is to see the effects of crowds on the underwater environment.

Remember, too, that although people have been going into the aquatic environment since there were people—swimming, diving for food, for shells, for pearls—the full-scale intrusion of divers into the underwater world is a very new phenomenon. Jacques Cousteau only co-invented scuba in 1943. Even more recent is our attempt to really understand the implications of this invasion, and how to control it.

Back in 1943, the whole concept of environmentalism was nonexistent. The war was going on. After the war came prosperity and expansion. Only in the early 1960s did an awareness of the effects of us humans on our own environment, the terrestrial environment, begin to grow. And it's only been within the last five or six years that people have begun to worry about the long-term effects of the human invasion of the aquatic environment.

Recently, on one of the many television cable channels that feature animals, I saw a show chronicling dives in Australia, off the Great Barrier Reef. In the course of the show several divers grabbed on to a large sea turtle. In a rhapsodic video vision, the divers hung on as the turtle flew through the water. Then, immediately afterward, the camera focused on the divers. One said that this had been the closest relationship she'd ever had with an aquatic animal. She said she was incredibly moved by it; it really showed that humans and animals can interact.

What really happened here?

Let's think about it from a different perspective. You're walking down the street in your hometown when suddenly a little ship lands next to you. The door pops open and out come huge bug-eyed creatures of nightmares—they've got teeth and big grins, and they're wearing helmets and all sorts of exotic equipment. *Uh-oh,* you think, feeling the old fight-or-flight response taking over.

But before you can run like hell, these things bound over to you and grab you by your shoulders. Belatedly, you panic! You go crazy with fear, and run. You run as fast as you can. The creatures are fairly light, though, and they're holding on to you, and they won't let go. You run and run and run until you're exhausted. Finally you stop and wait for the inevitable—death. The predator-prey relationship has been played out, and you're obviously on the losing side.

Then the creatures just let go, drop off, and wander back to their ship, where they shoot some home video footage and talk a bit about how they finally were able to relate to the warm-blooded animals in this terrestrial biosphere. If you could speak their language, you'd hear them say that the experience, the *relationship*, made them feel good and warm.

Okay, maybe that's a little Saturday-afternoon-matinee overwrought. But is it not, in fact, what we're doing? Is it not what happens when we go under water and try to ride a turtle, or a manta ray, or even the magnificent whale shark? From a human-centric standpoint, we've had a relationship with an undersea animal.

However, I would say that the undersea animal has not had a relationship with us. Very likely all we've done is induce fear, even panic, in the animal. We may have shortened its life, or damaged its ability to reproduce, or caused it to miss a reproduction cycle, or slightly tipped the delicate balance that allows it to deal with ocean predators. Maybe that individual animal was critical within its microenvironment. The fact is that we don't know what we've done; most of us have not spent our lives studying the behavior of undersea animals. We just don't have a clue.

I think it's amazing that even at this stage in our environmental awareness, good people can go diving, terrify the indigenous animals, and then suggest that the experience helped them understand the animals and their environment.

I wouldn't be dwelling on this so heavily if I didn't see similar practices depicted in every third television show on scuba diving. Scuba shows don't always feature the best diving practices. The focus of the show I just described was on environmental considerations in the ocean realm. It examined some fishing issues and looked at some of the new underwater nature preserves that promote tourism in developing nations. I've dived in areas that have been fished out and seen the barrenness there, and I agree about the value of creating preserves.

But at the same time, this and other shows perpetuate a misappreciation of the underwater realm. The other day, I heard an otherwise fine divemaster apologize to a group of American divers for not being able to find a manta ray large enough for them to ride. Every single diver there expressed his or her disappointment.

And that's where we come back to the uncertainty principle. The more we observe the underwater realm, the more changes come about from our observation.

Instead, we have to remember that the creatures that live under water are not like us. We tend to be more empathetic to creatures that are "like us." Puppies are cute; a panda bear cub can rend our hearts. In some of the most popular science fiction movies—the *Star Wars* trilogy, for example—the friendly aliens, the Ewoks and the Wookies, were carefully created to fit into our preconceived notions of what is "like us."

Most sea creatures, though, are the ultimate manifestation of "not like us." Why are we comfortable with dolphins? Why do dolphins play such a large role in our popular culture? I contend it's because we see them as "people of the sea"; because they've been presented in television and movies as "like us." They have language, they do tricks. These are the ocean creatures most like us—yet up until the last few years we've been willing to see hundreds of thousands of them killed by the tuna industry. What does that say for those creatures "not like us"? The now-endangered shark, for instance, or coral, which is after all a living, breathing organism?

When we enter the aquatic realm, we look around and see trees of coral, sea grasses, fish, turtles, and eels—and they see us. Think of those old black and white Tarzan movies in which the jungle is initially very noisy, with birds squawking, monkeys screaming, and lions roaring, until one human steps in. Suddenly, the jungle goes dead quiet. Because it is watching.

Well, we might not perceive all the interactions that are going on in the underwater world, but when we enter it, the "jungle" gets very quiet. The aquatic environment is a hard place, where predator and prey are locked in an endless dance. When we enter it, we bring with us the single biggest question of the jungle: Are we predator or are we prey?

And the environment begins changing, because they're watching us, just as we're watching them.

Another point to remember is that we actually know very little about the aquatic biosphere. The oceans cover 71 percent of the earth, but it's only been in the last three decades that research has focused on the consequences of humanity's relationship with the oceans.

As divers, it's important to remember that we still don't fully understand what natural cycles are at work under water. And in light of this lack of knowledge, the only environmentally ethical way to approach the underwater realm is conservatively. If we have a question about whether what we're doing is right, then we shouldn't do it.

What does this mean specifically? What we need is a set of ecological ethics for divers. It might include the following items:

1. To be as unobtrusive as possible, you must have absolute control of your buoyancy.

Beginner's scuba classes always focus on achieving neutral buoyancy—that is, hanging motionless in the water. But control of buoyancy is something you should focus on as a beginner, as an intermediate diver, and throughout your entire diving career. Every time you so much as touch a portion of the underwater environment, you risk destroying it. In the case of corals, even a slight touch can mean death. Coral has a tiny sheen of mucus that helps protect it from the environment, and one touch means irreparable damage. That single touch multiplied by two million divers can have a long-term effect on whole coral colonies.

Think of high alpine meadows, which may exist for only 60 days at the height of the summer. If you walk through one you'll destroy what little soil and nutrients are there. Footprints will stay for however long it takes that meadow to repair the damage—100 years or more. Coral colonies are similar. They can take hundreds of years to grow. It's heartbreaking to see divers dropping to the bottom and crashing into coral. But it's something that we can *directly* control.

2. You have an obligation as an environmentally ethical diver to see to it that the people you dive with are also in control of their buoyancy. If you see them being careless, don't yell at them, but be firm.

3. Minimize active encounters with aquatic life.

No riding the fish. Observe them, but don't interact with them in such a way that could be damaging to individuals.

When you see a fascinating form of sea life—a shell, a sea snail—fight the natural urge to pick it up and examine it closer. I find myself unwilling to pick up any shelled sea life, because I'm not sure what effect I'm having on this animal or its environment. I'd rather err on the side of caution.

I am also opposed to feeding fish to draw them in for divers. People are not allowed to feed bears in national parks; is shark so different? Feeding animals disrupts the food chain by pulling them away from the natural sources of food that they must continue to gather and eat to survive in a hostile environment.

In short, the underwater realm is not Disney World with fish. The first step in being an environmentally aware diver is coming to grips with this point.

3:
What the Other Guys Won't Tell You

ere's something a lot of people in the dive industry don't want you to know—diving is a *risk sport*.

What this means is that the consequences of making a mistake in diving can be severe. You can end up in a decompression chamber; you can end up with permanent damage, from chronic aches to paralysis. You can even die.

All this, though, isn't to say that diving isn't a safe sport. In fact, diving can be considered a safe sport.

So how are those two statements reconciled? That's an important question for people who are thinking about diving, or learning to dive. The answers shape the way we look at scuba diving. Unfortunately, because of hype within the industry, many of us have gotten the wrong impression of diving.

Let's take a look at risk and safety and how these elements apply to learning how to scuba dive.

First, what do we mean when we talk about risk? Unfortunately, we tend to use *risk* and *safety* interchangeably. For instance, we might say, "That's risky; that's not safe." Or, "That's very low risk, therefore, it's very safe."

When we talk about risk, though, what we're actually talking about is the *consequences of failure*. I learned this from mountaineers, people who spend a lot of time on big mountains. One of the things they've told me is the way they evaluate a climb or mountain: They look at it and say, "The risks on this mountain are higher, because the consequences of failure are higher."

I've also heard this definition of *risk* applied to whitewater rafting. When you go from a Class I (very moderate) rapids to a Class V (very extreme), what's the difference in risk? Well, as one rafter said to me, "If you fall out in a Class I rapids, you get wet. If you fall out in a Class V rapids, you get dead."

Risk increases, then, when the consequences of failure increase.

Safety, on the other hand, is calculated on an entirely different basis.

Typically, the safety of a sport is rated by the number of injuries per 100,000 participants (or the number of deaths per 100,000 participants). Based on these ratings, which are updated every year—and which actually mean absolutely nothing—scuba diving is very safe.

I once saw a presentation by a large dive agency in which it was said that you are more likely to be injured bowling than diving. Well, that's probably true in terms of injuries per 100,000. You carry a heavy bowling ball, your wrist gets sore, you get carpal tunnel syndrome, your fingers get strained, you drop the ball on your foot. But it's unlikely that you're going to die from bowling.

17

Diving may indeed have fewer injuries per 100,000 than bowling. The consequences of failure in diving, however, are much more severe.

So how do you evaluate these consequences? And how, then, does this change the way you look at scuba diving? Apply the same parameters to scuba diving that you would to any other risk sport, whether climbing, downhill mountain biking, or skydiving. Evaluate risk in diving as you would in any other sport that features severe consequences for failure.

Why is this an important aspect of learning to dive? Because when you focus on safety, as opposed to risk, you tend to downplay the very items that you need to pay the most attention to. For example, if you say, "This is a safe sport," there's a very human tendency to add, "Well, then, gee, I don't have anything to worry about."

Years ago, I was taking a dive course in a lake in central Florida. The subject was underwater navigation, and it involved spending a lot of time in murky, shallow water following a compass around. It wasn't very interesting, but I knew that navigation would be an important skill in my future dive training. On this particular day, we'd completed a whole series of dives—a day's work. We were 20 yards from shore—not even the length of an average swimming pool. One of my classmates surfaced, panic-stricken. She was waving her arms, short of breath—the classic panic symptoms. She shouted, "I'm going to drown!" Well, she couldn't drown: She had a fully inflated buoyancy control vest; she was surrounded by people within an arm's reach, most of whom were strong swimmers; she was 20 yards from shore. She was, in fact, very safe. After calming her down and helping her to shore, I debriefed her. She said she'd been under the impression that diving was a very safe sport, yet she'd still panicked. Obviously, the fact that diving is safe had nothing to do with her panic threshold. She felt that she'd been cheated: If this was so safe, why would she panic?

This is, unfortunately, one of the problems with what I think of as the old paradigm for scuba diving. What we've done over the last 20 years is overemphasize diving's safety in light of the total number of injuries versus the total number of participants in the sport. We've created a mindset in which safety is equated with "nothing bad can happen to me."

The reason the woman panicked was that there was no visibility. We were in a lake, and the water was very dark. The absence of light, the absence of any reference point, was terrifying to her. Focusing on the question "Is it safe?" overlooks the true question, which is "What are my real risks?"

When looking at diving as a risk sport, the first question that comes to my mind is, "What are my actual risks versus my perceived ones?"

And those two are almost never the same. It's one of the most interesting phenomena about a risk sport: Perceived risks and actual risks are not at all congruent. Sometimes they're not even in the same universe.

For instance, the first thing people think of when they think about diving in the ocean is that Bruce the Shark is going to eat them like canapés. It's all over; they're snack food, the human equivalent of cucumber sandwiches.

Well, the odds of that happening are minuscule. There have been shark attacks, certainly, but the number is tiny, and the risk equivalent to that of walking down the street on a bright sunny day and being struck by lightning. Yes, it's a risk, but more a perceived risk than a real one. The fear of ocean life is a primary perceived risk in diving, but a very small actual risk.

Still, worrying about hostile sea life can cause divers to focus on all the wrong things. I've been with divers on large boats in the Caribbean whose whole focus was on making sure they had at least two or three knives in case Bruce—or maybe one of those giant squids that Peter Benchley writes about, or a moray eel from their favorite James Bond movie—was about to attack them. They were ready, they explained to me, to fend off these demon creatures of the deep. And they could describe to me at great length the knives they'd purchased—I've heard the longest and most loving stories about dive knives you can imagine. They were ready but, like the panicky woman in the lake, they were ready for the wrong thing.

So if the giant shark is not the true risk factor, what is?

Real
Risks

The biggest risk factor in diving is carelessness. Carelessness leads to mistakes, which lead to panic, which has very unpleasant consequences.

Carelessness can take the form of failing to follow a dive plan, staying too long on the bottom, descending too deep, or ascending too quickly (which doesn't allow the body to decompress, or shed the nitrogen that was forced into its tissues by the increasing pressure).

Carelessness causes divers to exceed the limits of their ability or, worse, to not understand the limits of their ability. How dangerous can it be to go in one little cave, to crawl inside that one small wreck?

Carelessness can also come from maintaining equipment with the same laissez-faire with which most people maintain their bicycles or Rollerblades.

Carelessness sneaks up, and panic follows close behind.

None of this stuff is secret. There's also another big risk factor in diving, though. Most of the sport's serious problems are related to decompression. When you walk into your first open water class, one of the very first things you'll learn is that the reason for timing how long you stay on the bottom and how long you are actually under water is that your ascent speed is based on the amount of excess nitrogen that your body has absorbed during the dive. You must bleed that nitrogen out of your system—decompress—as you go back up. It's kind of ground zero for diving technique—as you go down in the water, your system absorbs nitrogen; as you come up, the natural tendency of nitrogen is to be reabsorbed into the bloodstream.

Thus, you have to ascend in a way that allows your body to out-gas that nitrogen. And if you stay at the bottom beyond a certain length of time you must go through decompression diving—stopping at certain levels to allow your body to out-gas nitrogen.

Failure to go through decompression properly is what causes divers the most trouble. It will be covered in detail in chapter 10.

So what can happen if you ignore all your charts and the $500 computer that you saved up all your money and robbed your kids' college fund to buy? What can happen if you go down, stay down, panic, and blow up to the surface?

Well, it's rare, but you can die. Quickly and painfully. Or you can find yourself transported in an emergency helicopter to a hospital, where you'll be placed in a decompression chamber—a sealed chamber in which you'll be recompressed then carefully "decompressed." You can suffer long-term damage, paralysis, pain, any number of bad consequences for ignoring this central risk factor. The bubbles of nitrogen, you see, can lodge in your body's joints and, through a process that's still the subject of some scientific vagueness, cause severe injury or even death.

The big question that comes to mind is, "Gee, if this is the danger point, why don't we just pay more attention to it? Why don't we focus so keenly on it that we eliminate the danger?"

Part of the answer is just human nature. Again, mountaineering provides us a good analogy. Within the mountaineering community risks are divided into two different types—subjective and objective.

What Is a Subjective Risk?

Basically, a subjective risk is one over which you have some control. A lot of risks can be ameliorated by the way you act, by the way you move, and by your training. For instance, if you're climbing a mountain and the weather's going to be very, very cold, then cold is a risk factor. Cold will kill you: You can freeze to death. You can reduce this risk factor, however, by the way you dress and prepare.

Similarly, in diving, environmental factors bring risk. If the water's very cold, you'll have to wear an exposure suit—but the suit will protect you. Cold is a subjective risk.

Another type of subjective risk in diving is panic. In fact, panic is a major part of almost all the other risk factors. It is an additive to other problems.

For example, if you're cold and you start to shiver, well, that's one thing. But if you're cold, you start to shiver, and suddenly you have a panic attack, then your situation has just gotten quantums worse. You've lost control.

That's why I say that panic is an additive factor in almost every situation. In fact, within the technical diving community—among cave divers and deep wreck divers, for instance—the general thinking is that panic is what will kill you 99 times out of 100. Because when you panic, your brain shuts down. And when your brain shuts down, even if you know what to do, what steps will resolve the situation you're in, you really can't act. You can't bring yourself to save yourself, because your brain is no longer functioning.

Panic is a classic subjective risk factor because it's *controllable*.

And how do you control it? Not by saying, "Gosh, I'm not going to panic," because it doesn't work that way.

Panic can be controlled with training. You train, learn, complete your open water certification, and then practice. Training and practice. Training and practice. Training and practice are the ways to deal with panic.

This isn't specific to diving; it's very common within all risk sports. In fact, the way police SWAT teams are taught to function in nightmarish situations is training and practice. They practice a new skill over and over again until it's virtually an automatic reflex.

The body-mind combination is pretty amazing. But it can't function at an optimum level unless a program is in place that allows the body to understand what it is the mind needs it to do. When you're under high stress, when you're panicky, is not the best time to determine what your needs are in a rational way. If you've trained and practiced, however, your mind and body will have a program to follow.

What's an Objective Risk?

An objective risk is one over which you have no control. In mountaineering, the classic objective risk is an avalanche. In scuba diving, an example of objective risk is equipment failure. Every diver I know has had well-maintained, high-quality equipment fail in use.

It happens. Anything people build can fail.

But there are still things you can do to protect yourself from objective risks. Let's go back to that avalanche. To protect yourself, you can learn the conditions that cause avalanches; you can learn where *not* to be, so if the mountain does fall it doesn't fall on you.

What do you do in the case of an equipment malfunction when diving?

You may need redundancy. For example, if your computer fails, you have a second computer. If your second computer fails, you have a watch. If your regulator—the device that delivers air from the tank—fails, you've got a backup.

And what about creatures that can eat you? Our pal Bruce the Shark, for instance, is another objective risk. You have no control over where a shark goes or what a shark eats.

You do have control over where you dive, though. You have control over the way in which you interact with creatures in the sea. You have control to, say, not swim with a pound of bacon strapped to your leg. Okay, that's a joke; still, in a lot of cases of dealing with objective risk, the obvious gets overlooked. And when you overlook the obvious, you put yourself at a much greater level of risk.

Nitrogen is also an objective risk. The way your body deals with gas is hardwired into your system. There's nothing you can do to actually change the way your body reacts to nitrogen.

There are things you must do to prepare yourself to deal with all of these risks. Thinking about what can fail makes people uncomfortable, though; it's easy to see why the dive industry hasn't wanted to use a risk-sport paradigm to analyze diving—the one in which you look at a sport and say, "If I do X, I will die." This tends to make you think, well, maybe I should stay home and watch the *Wide World of Sports* or that Discovery Channel special on white sharks instead. Maybe I should go bowling.

But people need adventure. And scuba diving is a way to bring adventure back into your life.

A risk-sport focus is important from the very first, because it will improve your diving. You'll learn something not because your open water instructor says you really need to know it, but because you'll understand *why* you need to know it.

Also, as you progress to more technical aspects of diving, starting from a risk paradigm means you have less to unlearn as you go. I've seen a number of divers—myself included—who in moving from open water or reefs into deep wrecks or caves have a lot of unlearning to do. Things we never before had to focus on all of a sudden take center stage.

Additionally, I have found that focusing on the risk factors initially has made me a calmer diver. Before every dive I've already asked myself "What if?" and already come up with a plan for dealing with it.

When I've had equipment fail, then, rather than panic I simply became annoyed, because I'd planned ahead and had backup. When my main computer failed at more than 130 feet once, I simply switched to my backup computer and terminated the dive. Another time, a rental regulator began free-flowing on me—that is, air began pouring out. I shut the regulator off, began breathing from my spare regulator, and terminated the dive.

Notice that any equipment failure, no matter how trivial, means the dive is over.

4:
The
Basics

When my partner and I began putting together *Over the Edge* magazine back in 1993, we started polling people informally on what outdoor sports they actually participated in, what sports they were really passionate about, and what sports they were sort of interested in, but in a secondary way.

One of the results that we found most interesting was that while virtually all of the people we talked to were certified divers, virtually no one listed diving as a passion.

This is not to say there aren't a lot of people who are passionate about diving; there certainly are. But it does show that the most active sportsperson, the one who is willing to try a number of different sports, tends to drift away from diving after a relatively short time.

That idea has held up in the statistics about scuba diving. While many people come into diving every year, many also go out.

Scuba diving has a very high dropout rate. In the course of writing this book I met a lot of people who were either certified to dive but didn't, or were once certified but got out of it.

I think I know some reasons for this softness within the dive market. The first is the way scuba has been presented for years: as something of an impulse sport. That really hit home with me recently when I went to a dive convention, a trade show open to the public. It was a regional show, and every dive shop in the area had its own booth. There were huge signs that read SHOW SPECIAL! LEARN TO DIVE! 3 DAYS; $100.

That's very much how the dive industry has presented itself over the years. The actual service it provides—the instruction—has become more and more a commodity, and its market increasingly price-driven. So you see intense competition. Dive shops working to get people in the door and signed up cut the price of certification. As they do so, they tend to cut their profit margins. As they cut margins, they have to skimp somewhere.

The cutbacks don't occur in the safety instruction, which is critical, but in other areas. For example, there are dive shops for which the sale of mask, fin, and snorkel packages (I'll discuss these more in chapter 6) *is* the margin. They are literally making no money on instruction. The instructors are making a small amount of money, but the shops themselves are profiting only from sales of instruction books, ancillary equipment, masks, fins, and snorkels.

The unfortunate thing about this type of situation is that it tends to put the instructors in a sales position. It isn't good for the dive industry when its most critical resource, its instructors, is turned into a commodity.

Divers are drawn into this commodity market as well: Get your certification, go to Cozumel, go to the Cayman, see blue fish, come home, forget about it.

In most other risk sports, you'll find a fairly well-paid instructor base. And they should be paid well, because they are teaching critical skills.

Within the diving community, however, the exact opposite has been the case. Only recently, with the rise in technical diving—diving beyond the range of recreational scuba—has the emphasis returned to high-quality instruction. Technical diving instruction, as compared to recreational scuba training, tends to be drastically more expensive. That's not because the instruction itself is expensive; it's because in recreational scuba, lessons are priced under their value.

A second reason for this softness in diver commitment is that recreational scuba divers often suffer from the "bird-watching complex." They are drawn to recreational scuba by the entrancing undersea environment. I was, certainly. Divers go to the Caribbean, or to some of the spots off Baja or Hawaii, for this reason. And it's exciting—until they go to the next place, and the next place, and the next. What tends to happen is diver burnout, which I call the "blue fish syndrome": Now that they've seen a blue fish in three or four different oceans, they've begun to lose interest.

You may argue, "Well, that's ridiculous. I can go on a hike and see the trees and the trail, and it's very beautiful. I go on the same hike the next day and see something entirely different."

But what happens is that people are drawn into diving with the perception that it is an adventure. Well, diving *can* be an adventure. It can also be excruciatingly dull. I've been on large dive boats in the Caribbean that I would classify as one step above, say, work release. They're crowded. There's no individual attention. There're too many people fumbling around who don't have a clue what they're doing. The dive-masters themselves are apathetic. They've taken your money only to get you into the water, get you out of the water, get you back on the beach, thank you, and wish you a good night.

This kind of experience turns a lot of people off diving. After the initial excitement wears off, after the thrill is gone, then people simply don't go on. They move on to a different sport.

But there are solutions. There are ways to approach diving that can affect whether you stay in it for the long run or give up after a year or two.

This chapter is a prerequisite for the prerequisites, of sorts: a list of things you need to think about, and do, before you choose a shop or class and get your first instruction.

Why Do You Want to Dive?

The very first question you want to ask yourself is, "Why do I want to learn to scuba dive?"

That seems pretty self-evident, doesn't it?

In my own view, and that of friends who own dive shops, though, it's not a question people always ask themselves. In fact, at one friend's West Coast shop, when that question comes up—"Why do you want to dive?"—some people are stumped.

Their answers have included: "Because I saw the ad in the paper"; "Because I saw *Sea Hunt* five times"; "I just got back from a James Bond movie and there were sharks and spearguns and I really want to do that."

The problem with not having a firm idea of why you want to dive is that you're very unlikely to be satisfied with the results after you do learn how to dive.

In many ways, sports are like business: If you don't have clear goals, you can never really be sure whether you've reached them. Or if you'd prefer a more literary reference, consider the line from *Alice through the Looking Glass*: "If you don't know where you're going, it doesn't matter which road you take."

In diving, which represents a large commitment of time and, regardless what people have told you, of money, you really need to know what your goals are and whether you've reached them. Or if those goals are even reachable.

Avoid Confusing Gadgetry with Progress

Okay, I can hear you saying it: "Yeah, yeah, yeah, get on with the good stuff." This is, of course, another aspect of the problem. Diving can become a gadget-driven sport, which is a typically American phenomenon. Just take a look at the mainstream dive magazines, which virtually shout from their pages, "Consume! Consume!" A lot of the shouting is couched in terms of making us better divers, and providing us the equipment that can help do so. The danger is in confusing the purchase of equipment with the movement toward a real goal. I've noticed in sports that the finest pieces of equipment always seem to be in the hands of people who use them the least. The most beautiful (and expensive) bicycles I've ever seen belong to people who don't ride very much. The best fly-fishing gear is inevitably in the hands of people who rarely fish. Even swimmers aren't immune. Go to the pool and see who's got the $50 swim goggles!

And scuba divers may be the worst of the breed.

This isn't actually a tirade against having nice gear. Quite the contrary. But often the quick fix of buying new gear becomes a substitute for the longer, more arduous path of training and practice. We want to *do* something, so we *buy* something. I can always tell the difference between a new piece of gear that moves me forward and a new piece that simply assuages a gnawing need to torment my credit card. New gear that works seems to fill a hole in my technique— as if it's always been there, only I'm just now noticing it. The other kind of gear always leaves a slightly sour taste in my mouth, like I've been suckered by the best con man I know— myself. That kind of gear rarely lasts past the second dive.

Set Goals

A goal-setting process can help with gear selection—if you know where you're going, you have a baseline for evaluating your real needs. You can plan gear purchases to help you reach your goals. It won't give you full immunity from gadget fever, but it will blunt some of the worst symptoms.

But goal setting can help in other areas as well. So, what's the best way to approach it?

I say, very simply. And you've already begun. For example, you're reading this book. This isn't a textbook; it's not a how-to-dive book. It's about how to think about diving and about what you want from your scuba diving career.

A friend of mine told me recently that what she really wants to do is dive reefs off every continent in the world. Well, that's an excellent goal. She knows what she wants. She knows where she's going. She can look at her maps and say, "Gee, Africa is going to be tough. There's a lot I need to do first"—not just in terms of diving skills, but also in terms of logistics. So she's created a multiyear—and multilayered—adventure. She's not a wealthy person. To accomplish her goal is going to take time, commitment, and creativity. Learning to dive is for her only the first step in living out this ongoing adventure. I believe she'll be able to stay in diving for years and years, because she has made the sport an adventure. And I believe that she'll accomplish her goal.

Another example: I've met a number of divers in the last couple of years who have become fascinated by the concept of deep wrecks. Wreck diving has always been a part of scuba, a long-term specialty of the Professional Association of Diving Instructors (PADI) and the National Association

33

of Underwater Instructors (NAUI)—both large certifying agencies.

But my friends' goals go beyond the easy wrecks. These are people who want to see wrecks that are not tourist attractions, wrecks that are not easily accessible, and some of the more famous wrecks, such as the *Wilkes-Barre* off Key West. The *Wilkes-Barre* is about 250 feet down. It's a very complex, dangerous dive. It's not impossible, but it's years away from the beginning diver. With the *Wilkes-Barre* as a goal, however, my friends have something to aim for, and a way of measuring their progress.

So if you too are fascinated by ships and shipwrecks, put together a program and write it down. "I would really like to dive to the USS *Wilkes-Barre,* the *Andrea Doria,* the USS *Monitor*"—the so-called crown jewels of deep wreck diving.

Then ask yourself, "What does this mean in terms of training? Of experience? What are the implications for my life?" When I toured the country after my recent book on extreme sports, *Over the Edge,* came out, one of the things I discovered is that while people may be totally goal-oriented at work, when it comes to their leisure time they tend to say, "I don't want all that goal stuff weighing on me." So what happens is that they're focused and happy in their work lives, but their leisure time falls through the cracks.

A question that continually came up was, "You know, I've got my open water certification, and I've been to Cozumel, I've been to Grand Cayman. Now what?" This question is one that should be answered *before* you get your certification.

You want to create an adventure. The author Walt Burnett once wrote, "Adventure is a human need." The great Helen Keller, I think, put it even better when she said, "Life is either a great adventure or it's nothing."

The boom in sports like scuba diving, white-water rafting, and adventure racing has happened because we crave adventure in our lives the same way we might crave chocolate. Without adventure, something is missing, and often we're not sure what it is. But ultimately we have to create our own adventures. Signing up for a dive class is a step, but only the first step.

Create a plan. So you're interested in the underwater environment. What's the first thing you do? Read, study? Look around, talk to friends who are divers? Sure. More than anything else, though, what you should do is listen to yourself.

When you first heard about diving and started reading about it in magazines, what was it that drew you? Was it the blue fish? There's nothing wrong with that. The important thing is to know why you want to dive.

Start with a blank piece of paper and write down what it is that attracts you to the underwater world. Then think about what kind of goals you'd like to set. What is it that you would really like to do with your scuba diving?

In my own expeditions, I have found that the factor that most kept me from accomplishing something I really wanted was the mental restrictions that I placed on myself— a "can't, shouldn't, wouldn't, couldn't" situation. And as I traveled with *Over the Edge*, one of the things I consistently heard from people was, "I really want to do X, but I can't."

There's that old saying that goes something like this: "Whether you say you can't or you can, you're probably right."

Let's get back to the goal of the *Wilkes-Barre*—250 feet down. This was, by the way, one of my own goals when I started seriously diving. I asked myself what I had to do to accomplish it. Then I made a list:

I needed to learn to dive.

I needed to learn to wreck-dive.

I needed to learn about wrecks.

You don't need a really detailed list at first, because as you'll find out, every prerequisite has a prerequisite. Make a classic outline, the kind you learned about in tenth-grade English. This outline will give you a way to structure your overall dive training plan.

Getting Certified

You've written your list. You've thought about diving. You've got goals in mind. What do you need to do to reach them?

I've got to get certified.

Good plan. But before you get certified, remember that prerequisites always have prerequisites. I'd like to suggest a couple of things that the large certifying agencies won't.

1. Learn to swim. Why? Well, there is a swimming requirement in most dive training. I think I had to swim the length of the pool, or something like that. Generally, though, this swimming is done with a buoyancy control device (BCD) and flippers. I suggest that if you are serious about diving, you need to be serious about being a proficient swimmer. The stronger a swimmer you are, the more comfortable you'll be in the water. I've found that knowing how to swim is a tremendous confidence builder when people move into the dive arena, because the water no longer frightens them.

In fact, the year before last I was talking to a top national dive instructor who could dog-paddle and "sort of" swim. He was (and is) a fine dive instructor and a fine diver. I told him that it wouldn't hurt him to spend some time with a Masters swim group or at the YMCA taking adult swim lessons. He laughed pretty hard at that.

But later that winter, off season, he found himself at the gym with some time on his hands, so he took swimming lessons "for the heck of it." Much later, I got a call. "Look," he said, "amazingly enough, you were right. Swimming really gave me a whole different perspective in the water. I always thought I was comfortable in the water, but now I *really* am."

Swimming just gives you one less thing to worry about; it's not something you're necessarily going to use. I've never shucked all my equipment and swum to shore. However, when you start diving, little weird fears can gnaw at you. On one of my very first boat trips, I remember looking at the shore and saying to myself, "I could swim to there. I could get out of this boat and swim to there." And it made me feel a little more comfortable.

Anything you can do to ease the transition to open water is good. You may have practiced again and again in the pool, but open water is disconcerting. There are currents, different temperatures, waves. So it's wise to have done a few open water swims in a lake before diving.

If you need to learn or brush up on your swimming, I suggest the YMCA, which usually has basic adult swimming programs. Your focus should be on distance swimming, not sprinting.

2. A second prerequisite, which I've touched on briefly, is: Talk to people who dive. Ask them questions. Ask them annoying questions. How do you meet these people you plan to pester? Well, not by walking down the street and asking folks, "Hey, you dive?" Instead, overhearing a conversation, or meeting someone wearing a dive T-shirt from an area you might be interested in, is a good way. I've been pretty uninhibited about stopping people and striking up conversations: "Oh, did you go to this area? What was it like?"

But if you're not interested in buttonholing strangers, there're a couple of other options. Most areas have a dive club. You can find out by calling a dive shop in your area. Ask, "Is there a local dive club, and can I attend a meeting?" Just talking about diving is going to help you focus on your goals.

Another arena for conversation is online dive forums. It's easy to find them. Try any of the recreational scuba forums on the Internet. America Online, the largest online service in the country, has a huge divers' section. You can actually get online and chat with other divers, even other new divers, which is very helpful. At first you might want to "lurk"—read the messages without responding, or open some of the folders and read the long list of exchanges to get a feel for what people are talking about. You don't necessarily have to participate. Still, doing so can help you understand what the diving world is like, and introduce you to the range of people out there and what it is they're doing.

Which will help you focus on what it is that you want to do.

A quick online caveat—remember that 99.9 percent of what you read is *opinion*, not fact. Just because someone (even me) says so emphatically doesn't make it a fact.

3. A third important prerequisite, which a lot of folks like because it invites poking around and checking out gadgets, is to spend some time hanging around dive shops. Talk to instructors and veteran divers. And remember, they're going to be pitching you. If you're considering taking dive lessons, they want you. So they're going to be putting their best foot forward. Frequent several dive shops. Ask questions. "I'm thinking of instruction; give me a little background on your shop." (How to choose an instructor will be covered in the next chapter.)

    When I started out, I did exactly the wrong thing. I picked the dive shop closest to my house, walked in, and signed up. A little-bitty hole-in-the-wall shop. An old service station with a couple of masks on the wall.

    It ended up working out fine. Luckily enough, the instructors were excellent. But I think my diving career would have progressed a lot quicker had I done a little research.

    So look at the shop. How does it look? New, modern? Or like the Black Hole of Calcutta? A lot of different equipment for sale? Good selection? Look around for a list of trips. What are they doing? Where are they going? Look at the range of instruction offered.

    These days the pressure is on dive shops to try to find a way to make soft divers—"Well, I dive a little; so what?"—into serious, ongoing consumers of dive goods, dive travel, and dive services.

The really good shops are two steps ahead of their students in instruction: By the time you think you might want the instruction, there's already a class.

Certifying Agencies

What's a certifying agency? There are a number of agencies in the United States that train and certify new divers. They give you a certification card, or C-card, which allows you to get your scuba tanks filled. I hesitate to put a finite number on how many certifying agencies there are at this minute—it's a growth industry. The largest is PADI, with NAUI close on its heels. There's also SSI, Scuba Schools International, along with the YMCA—which, in fact, was the first agency to offer scuba certification in the United States.

One of the newest open water dive certification agency is the International Association of Nitrox and Technical Divers, or IANTD, which has moved into the open water arena from the technical in order to offer a full range of services. Then there are specialized certifying agencies, primarily in the technical arena—Technical Divers International, Professional Scuba Association, and others.

How do you choose?

The truth is, it doesn't matter. Every one of the agencies that certifies for open water will offer you fine instruction. Each has different programs, but all are similar in scope. And I will wager that if you see diving as a lifetime adventure, along the way you are going to end up with certifications from a lot of different agencies. I have a stack of certification cards myself from nearly all of them.

Still, you have to begin somewhere. So as you flip through the phone book and see listings for a NAUI agency, a PADI agency, an IANTD instructor, realize that the agency itself is less important than your relationship with your future instructor. That's what I'll talk about in the next chapter.

5:

How to Instruct an Instructor

et me start by getting you off on the wrong foot. The scene that follows is how too many people choose their scuba diving instructor.

Cut to a store, big store, masks on the wall, tanks lying against the wall, a lot of folks sitting around the outdoor pool. There're a couple of people crawling around the bottom of the pool, bubbles coming up. In walks the potential new student, right up to somebody sitting by the pool, and asks, "Are you a dive instructor?"

Person by the pool nods his head. "Yes, I'm a dive instructor."

Potential student says, "Cool, how much does it cost?"

Guy sitting by the pool responds, "Hundred fifty plus books."

Newcomer says, "Cool, where do I sign up?"

Well, that works. It's good for the shop, because it didn't have to work very hard to reel you in. But you're not taking full advantage of the knowledge that's out there.

David Feeney—a dive shop owner, divemaster, and friend—says the single most important thing for a potential new student to learn about diving is what questions to ask an instructor.

"If you don't interview the instructor," Feeney says, "how do you know what you're getting? How do you know you're getting what you're paying for?"

Five Essential Qualities of a Good Dive Instructor

Whether you're looking for a climbing instructor, a sky-

diving instructor, or a scuba instructor, there are five qualities that all good ones share.

1. Most important is a *focus on safety*. This is critical in
   diving. Safety has got to come first, second, third. It has
   to be the central focus of any dive instructor (or any
   high-risk-sport instructor).

   How can you tell if an instructor has a focus on
   safety? He or she will tell you that very quickly. With
   the best instructors I've ever worked with, the first or
   second sentence out of their mouths was about
   safety: that safety was going to constantly be the
   watchword.

   You can also ask your potential instructors what
   they do to focus on safety. Or you can observe a class.

   In a dive class, there's a very clear line between
   having fun and horsing around. I have seen some open
   water classes that were very lax in discipline. The
   instructor didn't seem to pay nearly as much attention
   as I felt was warranted. Good instructors always pay
   close attention to the students; sometimes they seem to
   have eyes in the back of their heads. They head off any
   situation that might conceivably be unsafe. Classes
   should be fun, but disciplined, and there should be no
   question who is in charge.

   An instructor with a safety focus will very quickly
   correct your misperceptions about safety issues. I've had
   high-end instructors stop me while I was in the middle
   of explaining what I wanted to do and tell me that I was
   thinking about it wrong, that I would be creating a
   potentially unsafe situation. And that while they certainly wouldn't stand in my way, they wouldn't help me,

either, unless I was willing to reconsider a safer approach. A sign of a good instructor is one who will stop you and say, "You need to do it a different way, because that's the safest way."

2. The second essential quality of a good scuba instructor is *patience*. When students start out, they all have questions—thousands of questions. And an instructor has heard every one of those questions thousands of times before. Nevertheless, it's key that the instructor be able to listen patiently and answer patiently: Doing so alleviates beginners' fears and uncertainties about diving.

As a not particularly patient person myself, I have a tremendous respect for instructors who achieve that necessary level of the quality. For example, in the time Wings Stock spent instructing me (a thankless job, to be sure) in technical diving, he showed amazing tolerance in the face of an incredible list of stupid questions—although I do subscribe to the theory that the only stupid questions are the ones you don't ask. Of course, about the fifth time I asked him to re-explain how to use a certain formula, he probably secretly wanted to smack me over the head. A good instructor must be patient, willing to explain, and willing to go into detail to get to the very bottom of your inquiries.

3. An instructor must also have *breadth of knowledge*. Instructor training is a long, arduous process designed to ensure that the candidate has a complete background in and knowledge of diving, along with the ability to convey that knowledge to another person. An argument can be made that anybody who has made it to the instructor level has knowledge.

But I like to see something more. I like to see instructors who have the desire to keep learning. It's important that dive-service consumers realize the entire scuba industry is evolving. The sport of diving is changing, at this point, on a virtually daily basis. The best instructors are aware of this and are themselves students, learning as things change. I don't think there's an instructor in the country who'll claim to know it all. Continued learning, continued knowledge, continued training help instructors become better instructors, because they are always students as well.

The very best instructors are able to take the problems they experience as students and translate them into solutions for their own pupils. This ability is perhaps more common in the martial arts than in any other type of sports instruction. Within some martial arts, there's very little difference between student and instructor. To move through the ranks, each student must teach. Learning and teaching are tied together; "student" and "instructor" are part of the same continuum.

So when you look for knowledge in an instructor, look for someone who is pushing his or her limits, learning new things, and keeping up with the developments in scuba.

4. Along with the exuberant search for knowledge comes the fourth critical factor, *enthusiasm*.

I want an instructor who's excited about being a diver, and excited about teaching other divers, and can transfer that enthusiasm to students.

The worst instructors are the ones who have been instructors for a long time and are bored, bored, bored. Everybody I know has encountered an instructor like this. Luckily, it doesn't describe the majority of dive instructors, but there are people out there for whom the diving career is just another day at the office. These are not the people you want to get your training from.

Enthusiasm leads to inquisitiveness, which leads to better ways of teaching. One of the dangers of a very large organized sport like diving is that teaching methods become institutionalized. Fortunately, this is changing. The larger certifying agencies are responding to the market and going back to look at the way they've taught diving. Up until a few years ago, the sense I got was, "We've been doing this for years, and we've got it down." That's never the case. You've never got it down. There is always a better way.

Enthusiastic, inquisitive instructors continually question their own knowledge base and methods of teaching, and are always asking, "How can I make this better, more understandable, easier for my students?"

5. The final critical quality in any instructor might be called *attitude*, but it's really more than that. A mountaineer friend of mine defines what she calls the instructor's mentality. Say you're climbing a mountain and all of a sudden there's an earthquake, then a volcanic eruption, then a tidal wave. The true instructor will say, "Well, that's interesting." The key here is an unflappable personality, someone who doesn't raise his or her voice unless you're about to kill yourself.

An instructor's mentality is one that immediately puts you, the student, at ease. As soon as you talk to your potential instructor, you should feel comfortable. You should find yourself almost reflexively wanting to trust this person. Which, of course, is exactly what you have to do with an instructor.

The perfect instructor, then, is a combination of all five critical attributes. Ideally, an instructor is always a step ahead of you, getting ready to answer your question before you've actually framed it. An instructor is always trying to show you a clear path. An instructor is unlikely to be ruffled. An instructor has planned in advance for any problems that might come up, can answer your questions, can handle your emergencies, and can show you things that you would not, on your own, see.

Questions for Your Instructor

Given the five critical qualities listed above, you can probably guess what these questions are going to be.

1. *How long have you been instructing?* Does this imply that people who have been instructing longer are better instructors? Not necessarily. But if you're looking for instruction in a high-risk sport, it should be from somebody with at least a couple of years on the job. Why? Because school is not like the real world, and instructor training is like school. Yes, the goal is to make sure the new instructor is ready for the real world. I still like an instructor to have a couple of years' seasoning before I sign up.

As you move through open water courses into specialty areas and beyond, you'll want more and more experience in each specialty from your instructors—and you'll most likely find it. The diving community is still relatively new, and as a result you may have the opportunity to train with some of the people who helped define the sport. It's a little like having Richard Petty give you driving lessons. Take advantage of this.

If you have a choice between two instructors you like equally well, go with the one with more experience.

2. The second question follows from the first: *Of the classes I want to take, how many have you taught?* Sometimes upper-level scuba instructors will, for one reason or another, return to teaching Open Water I. Sometimes this works well; sometimes not. I hate to be a guinea pig myself. Whether it's a software program or a scuba course, I don't want the beta test version.

3. *What specialty classes do you teach?* This is a double-edged question—a sneaky way of addressing breadth of knowledge. If it turns out that you really like the instructor, this will tell you if there's a way you can work with him or her over the long haul. For example, David Feeney teaches a number of different classes and has students who have been with him for years. They move up in their scuba careers in classes that he teaches or on trips that he leads. In an ideal world, your instructor will be with you for a long time.

4. Another way to judge breadth of knowledge is to ask, *What sort of advanced dive training have you been doing?* And what is the potential instructor planning on doing in the near future? Is the shop looking into bringing in advanced dive training if it hasn't done so already?

You'll find out how enthusiastic a potential instructor is; and you'll learn whether a shop is on top of technology, trying to expand its offerings and encouraging its instructors to get out there and learn more. All of these are very good signs.

5. *Which trips have you guided? Where have you gone? Tell me a little bit about your last trip.* Find out how many people were on the trip and, of those participants, how many were return students. Ask how many were people the instructor trained. Ask if this was a regular or a first-time trip. Find out how many trips the company offers, and how many of those the instructor led.

6. *As an instructor, what are the specific areas that interest you?* Find out what sort of dives the instructor makes for fun. Wildlife watching? Wreck diving? Night diving? Deep diving? Treasure hunting?

   This is important to you because, as you will see later when I talk about advanced dive training, it will tell you whether your initial instructors are familiar with the area you want to focus on.

   Remember your diving goals. Ask yourself, when you're interviewing your instructor, "Is this somebody who can help me move toward them?" This is not to say that an instructor who's solely interested in wildlife can't help you become a really good wreck diver. But I can tell you, from experience, that if your goal is advanced wreck diving, an instructor who shares that focus can bring you up to speed much faster than one whose focus is on wildlife.

7. There's a final question I like to ask that's much like one

of those dumb questions you always get on job applications. *What's your dream dive?* Or, *What's your personal goal?*

Frankly, I would not sign up with an instructor who looked at me and said, "I've done everything," or "I just teach," or "the dive I did yesterday." Those are not good enough answers. One of the five essential qualities is inquisitiveness. Instructors who aren't focused on their own goals, as well as instructing, are not going to be as good as those expanding their horizons.

Hal Watts, one of the fathers of modern deep scuba diving—the man who coined the phrase "Plan your dive, dive your plan"—has been on the cutting edge of scuba for decades. But when you sit on his front porch and talk to him, you never get the sense that he feels he's done everything. Instead, you find yourself talking to someone who can't wait to get out on his next dive, who can't wait to go from open-circuit scuba to rebreathers, and who has more places and special dives on his list of things he wants to do than he could possibly have time for, even though his list of accomplishments is already stunning.

That's what I want in an instructor.

Set up your questions in such a way that you come away knowing whether you're willing to trust your life to this instructor. If that sounds dramatic, remember that scuba is a risk sport. If you're comfortable saying, "I'll put my life in this person's hands," you've found your instructor.

Instructors to Avoid

The flip side of finding the right instructor is learning to recognize the wrong instructor.

Yes, folks, they're out there. And, sure, what follows is gratuitous generalization. But take a good look when you visit dive shops, and I'll bet you'll stumble across some of these people. For better or for worse, here's who to avoid:

1. *The scuba dude.* You can immediately recognize the scuba dude, because he's wearing sunglasses that cost more than your car. He's laid back in that old-cool sort of way: "Been there, done that, got a tan."

   You're likely to find dudes down in the Caribbean. Generally, they've come out of resort training. (This is a subject in itself, and one I won't be addressing in this book. If you're going to learn to dive, take a course from a reputable dive shop, not a one-day course at a resort.) Ask a scuba dude a question and you'll get a lot of smiles, a lot of vague answers, a lot of suntan oil, and phrases like, "Whatever you want to do, little lady, I think we can help you."

2. *The faux–navy SEAL instructor.* This is the guy who owns every piece of equipment in the world, and it's all in black. The one who has a dive knife the size of your average machete. Many of these instructors did come out of military training, and military dive training is probably as good as it gets—hard, tough, and nasty. But it's not unusual to come across "military-style" instructors without real military credentials. Lots of discipline and no entertaining of questions. And even if the information they give is correct, the students don't necessarily absorb it, because they're busy trying to figure out how to keep from being yelled at or made to look like a dolt.

   If you can find a legitimate ex-SEAL instructor, sign up immediately and gut your way through the course. But ask for credentials.

3. *The Princess (or Prince) of Ennui.* You say to her, "I'm really interested in this." The automatic response is, "Yeah, I did that in '82." You say, "I'd really like to dive here," and she says, "Well, I dove that in '89." The key phrase from the Princess is, "Yeah, I did that," delivered with a pained sigh in her voice. The implication, of course, is that you should have been here in '82, or '89, or whenever, back when it mattered.

Right.

4. A fourth type of instructor that David Feeney warns about is a variant of Sergeant Rock. This is the *I Crossed Borneo with a Knife in My Teeth and a Babe on My Arm and a Cigarette in My Mouth and Survived–type dive instructor.* These are the instructors who, as soon as you have the misfortune to set foot in their shop, say such things as, "Oh man, you're going to have such a great time! Just last week in my Open Water I class, I was almost ripped apart by a man-eating shark, but at the very last minute I was able to pull out my Swiss Army Knife, drive it into his weak spot just in front of the dorsal fin, and scare him away."

He'll ask what kind of diving you're interested in. If you say wreck, you'll hear, "Oh man, just last week I dove on this wreck, it was incredible. A huge piece of metal ripped my air system off and I was barely able to escape with my life. And that's not even counting the moray eel!"

David Feeney's rule of thumb is to never purchase instruction from anybody who tells you ridiculous war stories. He considers this an absolute rule. The first time someone comes up with an I Defy Death story, he's out of there. And I think you should be, too.

Why is that? How about bad karma? There are people out there who are ill prepared and ill suited for the demands of their sports. And the adventures they have occur not because of the sport itself but because they screwed up and didn't die.

That's the last thing you want from an instructor.

6:

Equipment
Basics

What is the single most important factor to consider when choosing equipment for scuba diving?

That's an easy one. Of course the answer is that all the colors you have match. Your wet suit needs to match your buoyancy compensator (BC). Your BC needs to match your fins. Your weight belt needs to be . . . well, accessories are everything. And let's not forget that mask. The last thing in the world you want is a mask that doesn't match your outfit.

Okay, okay—but as silly as this sounds, it's often the way scuba gear gets purchased.

I was on a boat a year or so ago with a guy who was in his first year of diving. He hadn't been on many dives. He had a yellow and black wet suit, a yellow and black mask, yellow and black gloves, yellow and black fins. His tanks were black with a yellow safety shield. He even had a dive watch in exactly the colors of his wet suit and accessories. I was so impressed. So I asked what criteria he had used to pick his dive gear, and he looked at me as though I'd come from another planet. "Well," he said. "Just look at it. Isn't this great?"

As it happened, his gear was very good. But his primary concern had been how he looked, not how the gear worked.

Fortunately, dive gear generally is made pretty well. Unlike the case of other types of sporting equipment, most of the brand-name dive gear will get the job done.

Most of us who have been diving for a while have a really interesting space in our houses called the dive closet, the junk closet, or the little room in the garage that everyone but us is afraid to go into. What's in this space is gear we've purchased that may have done the job for a while, but then stopped. Or—more accurately—as we progressed as divers, the gear that we purchased early on became obsolete.

There's nothing wrong with this. It's certainly good for the gear manufacturers. The problem is that it takes a lot of money. Every piece of gear that ends up in the closet or garage cost money that you can no longer spend to take a dive trip. It's money that's not being used to fill your tanks, or to get you to Cozumel, or the Red Sea, or—to pay the rent.

So when you start acquiring dive gear, one of the things you should keep in mind is, "How do I avoid the little room in the garage?"

Your first *real* question, however, is, "Where do I get this stuff, anyway?"

I want to make an impassioned plea for the retail dive shop. Now, a lot of you just flinched, because you thought you felt the wind created by money whipping out of your wallet.

It's true that retail dive shops charge more than mail-order houses. So why go to a retail dive shop?

Reason one is advice. Generally speaking, the people who work in dive shops are divers (if they're not divers at the shop you visit, pick another shop). What a retail dive shop offers is a very high concentration of expertise: instructors, people involved in every arena of diving, men and women who have been diving for decades. By dealing with a retail shop and paying its prices, you also buy the privilege of tapping its collected brains. Right now, this may not seem as important to you as saving a couple of hundred dollars, but as you progress as a diver it will become critical.

I often find myself calling my friend David Feeney, the owner of a Scuba Network shop in Brooklyn, to ask his opinion on a piece of gear. And his opinion is very valuable. If he doesn't have one, someone in his shop or someone he's been diving with probably does. That's worth more than the two or three hundred dollars you'll save by ordering every single piece of your gear from mail-order houses.

Reason two is that it's also important for you to establish a relationship with the local shop that goes beyond advice. Indeed, most local dive shops have already moved toward providing more than simply basic scuba instruction.

The aforementioned David Feeney runs regular trips around the world. Most larger dive shops offer such trips. And it's a real advantage to take these with people you know, partly because of the advice they can offer, and partly because it tends to be more fun. If you've done a lot of traveling to foreign countries, remember your very first solo trip. I'll bet you'll agree that having a group of like-minded people along would have been a tremendous help.

If you're getting ready to take your first trip to a foreign country, and it's going to be a dive trip, I can guarantee it will be easier if you travel with people you know.

Local dive shops also offer advanced instruction. Most dive shops now know which way the wind is blowing: toward increased scuba instruction. No matter where you live, you can most likely find a shop to take you from open water diving to advanced open water diving to the specialties and beyond.

There have always been what are called dive specialties. These are the niche classes. Traditionally, you could take short classes in wreck diving, night diving, rescue diving, and drift diving. But dive shops are now going beyond these.

An example is the trend toward nitrox—oxygen-enriched air. Big dive shops took the lead in providing instruction in and tanks filled with nitrox, and now the large certifying agencies have followed. More and more shops are going beyond recreational scuba into mixed-gas and more

technically oriented dive instruction. I am a strong proponent of continued dive education, and the easiest and most
cost-effective way to get that education is through a local
shop.

A fourth reason to buy at a local dive shop is that with
all the advice and access to training it can give you, the shop
may not be as expensive as it first seems. When you buy from
mail order, you've got to pay shipping. If there's a problem
with the equipment, you have to send it back to the manufacturer (as opposed to having it repaired or exchanged on
the spot). And when you need to have your equipment
repaired or serviced—the regular servicing of your regulator,
for instance—you're going to have to find a local shop to do
it anyway. If you're on a long bicycle ride and your chain
breaks, you can walk home; not so with scuba gear. It has
been my experience that local shops are less than thrilled to
repair and maintain equipment that they didn't sell. I
blanched when I read in a dive magazine recently that yard
sales were a good place to find cheap equipment, which
could then be rebuilt by a local shop.

A risk sport is not a place for a price-first shopping mentality. Instead of saying "scuba regulator," try saying "life-
support system." All of a sudden the line "I'm looking for a
cheap life-support system" sounds silly.

In addition, the cost of equipment has really come
down lately. Often retail shops offer package deals: a specific
regulator, BC, tanks, and instrumentation priced together.
The cost of some of these packages rivals that of a generic
package from a mail-order house.

A final reason to buy from a retail shop is that you can
actually see the equipment you're purchasing. You can handle it; you can feel the weight of it. In the case of a BC or
wet suit, you can check the fit. Different brands have differ-

ent fits, so it's a big advantage to be able to try this gear on. Some retail shops have pools or access to pools, and you can ask if they have any equipment that you can demo in the pool.

So now that you've decided to go to a retail store to purchase this equipment, get out your credit card and get ready for that first purchase.

When you sign up for your first open water class, you will be told that you need mask, fins, and snorkel. They're going to be your first scuba purchases. If your class is being offered by a retail store, it may have a snorkel, mask, and fin package available, usually at a low price. Well, as much as it pains me and your credit card to tell you this, that's not generally the best deal for you to take.

The mask, fins, and snorkel offered as a package deal for new students is intended to ease the expense burden, which is an admirable goal. What a retail outlet doesn't want is a potential student to come in, look at the cost of the course, plus the cost of the equipment, plus the cost of the book, and suddenly run out screaming to take up something inexpensive, like golf.

But think of it this way—your very first exposure to the underwater world is going to be through the mask, fins, and snorkel that you purchase at the beginning. I've talked to a number of students who'd purchased really inexpensive masks and never understood why they leaked all the time.

One in particular asked me how she could get her mask to stop leaking, because, she'd noticed, my mask never seemed to. Well, her mask cost $14.95 and mine cost $100.

I was very lucky. When I was getting ready to start my scuba classes, my friend David Feeney happened to be visiting. He said, "Why don't I take you to buy your mask, fins, and snorkel?" I thought this was great—free advice, good equipment. At the time, I was fairly broke. More than anything else, I wanted to get through the whole experience without having to hold up a liquor store for money.

So we went to several retail stores, until David found one that he felt met his standards. Right in front of us was a huge rack of masks, fins, and snorkel sets; all the way over on the left was a sign that read $19.95 A SET SPECIAL. All the way over on the right was a sign that read $130 A SET. Not knowing any better, I headed left: it made sense to me in my impoverished state. David, however, broke to the right. Watching him, I moved from $19.95 to $29.95 to $39.95 and stopped at $49.95.

"What do you think?" I asked. His exact word was, "Junk."

Eventually I followed him down to the $99.95 section, and he was able to fit a mask to my face. It was the single ugliest mask on the rack. With all these bright colors and all these neat-looking styles—some looked like they'd been splatter-painted, some were neon-colored—the mask David chose for me was ugly and gray. And expensive.

The snorkel? "Whatever snorkel comes with it," my mentor said. The snorkel was also gray. Ditto the fins.

I dutifully paid $99.95 for the set (made by Maris, by the way). Years later, on one grim afternoon, the mask vanished in an Atlantic storm. I still use the fins, and they are still the finest pair I've ever owned. I've replaced the mask with another Mares-style mask, also gray. It's a $99.95 set of equipment that I've been able to amortize over the better part of a decade. It's still ugly. But it does work extremely well.

Masks

You'll need someone at the shop to show you how to fit the mask to your face. (Basically, you put it on and push it a little to create some suction. Then bend your head forward and see if it stays on.) The best way to fit a mask is in a pool.

If you wear glasses or contact lenses, there are some other mask issues you should address up front. There are many masks available that can be fitted with prescription lenses. If you wear glasses on a regular basis, this is pretty much the only option open to you.

I would suggest strongly, however, that if you feel you need a mask with prescription lenses, you purchase a second backup mask, also with prescription lenses. Never forget Murphy's Law. I can guarantee you that if you have only one prescription mask, on your very first trip to a major dive site, or trip out of the country, or trip of your lifetime, you will lose that mask. And there you'll be, blind in paradise. It's going to be an initial expense, but one that will serve you well in the long run.

As an alternative, there are contact lenses. Some recent articles have stated that contact lenses are contraindicated for diving; I have never found that to be the case, though, nor have I ever run across an experienced diver who had problems with them. The certifying agencies also concur. I use Johnson and Johnson disposable contact lenses and have throughout my diving career. The advantage of these lenses—and it's a pretty big one—is that if my mask floods and I lose a lens, as soon as I get back to the boat I can pop in another set. They're cheap and I keep numerous pairs available. On long trips, especially trips out of the country, I take boxes of the little suckers. I will say, though, that in my years of diving, I've flooded my mask dozens of times, both by accident and in training. I can only remember losing one contact lens.

I've also used contact lenses on dives as deep as 250 feet, and on mixed-gas dives, without any problems.

mask

Another mask issue arises for all us old people—that is, people over 40. There's no denying or getting around it: After the age of 40, you start losing your ability to read up close. That's why we old folks all have reading glasses. But it's a big concern in diving, because you *must* be able to read your instruments while you're under water. Water does provide some magnification, so you'll find you can head the problem off for a while. But sooner or later, if you're going to continue diving, you must address this problem.

It actually happens pretty quickly. I used the same mask for years until one day, on a particularly deep dive—I think it was a 180-foot dive in a spring in Florida—I looked at my equipment and realized I was having trouble reading the smaller numbers. Up to that point, I really hadn't noticed it as a problem. This time, however, I found that while I could read the main numbers off my computers, the smaller numbers—the readouts giving me the depth and temperature— were blurs.

You can place small inserts—in effect, magnifying glasses—on the inside of your mask to allow you to see the instrumentation. Or you can get a dedicated mask that has the same feature in it. I use Sea View dedicated masks, which have the same fit as my old Mares mask (although in different styles) but also allow me to read the instrumentation.

Masks with built-in "reading glasses" take some getting used to: You need to look at a specific portion of the mask to read your instrumentation. If you need this sort of mask, be sure to get a feel for it in the pool first. If you're older and changing to a mask with a magnifying area, I would suggest making a couple of easy dives to start with; don't jump into a dark, deep, spooky dive with a piece of equipment that you haven't used. Even something as simple as a mask.

Snorkels

As diving becomes more technical, the trend is away from snorkels. Within the technical diving community, some feel that snorkels are an impediment. Among cave divers, they're just something else to get tangled up. When I started diving, I tangled a snorkel in a piece of wreck and peeled my mask right off. End of snorkel. End of dive.

However, in your initial open water training you'll be required to have a snorkel. And I can think of a couple of dives in rough water far from shore on which I did find myself using my snorkel. But you don't want to invest a huge amount of money in a water-free, nuclear-powered snorkel. Learn how to use a simple curved-tube model. Learn how to clear the thing. It's not a very big deal.

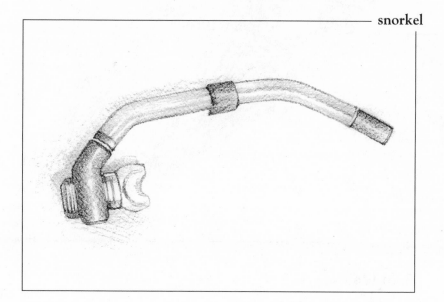

snorkel

Fins

Fins are a fairly personal thing. My tendency is to say larger is better—because, basically, it's going to give you more of a bang for the same expenditure of muscle energy. A smaller fin requires you to kick more or harder, and that's tiring. One of the things that you want to be in the water is relaxed. As you become a more accomplished diver, you'll want to expend as little energy as possible. Larger fins help with that. Just a little stroke with the fins, and you'll move right along.

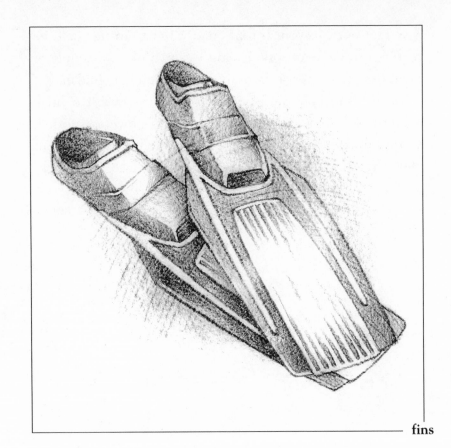

fins

Booties

One of the things that's generally not included in your first scuba package is a pair of booties—but you do need to wear them with most fins. As to the type of booties, ask your shop owner (start cashing in on the advice early). It depends on where you're diving. In Florida, get the thinnest—and cheapest—booties you can find. For colder water, get thicker models.

booties

I think I still have my first pair of booties; they're pretty ratty, but they work. If you plan to make a lot of dive trips on boats, you might want to look into the booties that are treaded. It's a little slippery on the boat, and the more tread you have, the better. Booties will add about $15 to the cost of your gear.

7:

Equipment Strategizing

Your basic gear—mask, fins, snorkel—will get you through your initial open water training. In fact, if you purchased wisely, this gear will get you through much of your career as a diver.

But let's say you've gone through your training, and you're looking at those next purchases. What should they be?

You'll need a breathing system, which includes the part of the regulator that connects to the tank and the part you breathe from. You'll also need a spare, or second, regulator. Other items include instrumentation; a buoyancy control device, which is the inflatable vest used to support your equipment; an exposure suit of some sort; and a whole slew of smaller parts, from tanks to knives to zip-ties.

But before you purchase, strategize.

What we're going to look at in this chapter is how to arrange your purchases in the most efficient and cost-effective way. At this point in your dive career you may be saying, "I've been using rental equipment, and I want to move up to my own gear. I really like this style [or brand, or whatever]. So what now? What kind of strategy do I need to come up with a set of scuba gear that I can feel comfortable with and travel with and that won't end up in the Equipment Black Hole downstairs? What do I need to get and in what order do I need to get it?"

Of course, if you happen to be someone like a country music superstar friend of mine, just call any big company and ask it to deliver, as he put it, "the whole kit and caboodle." The colors matched his tour bus and Harley Davidson, of course.

If you're like the rest of us, singing them old money blues, you're going to have to purchase your gear in stages.

Let's take these one at a time.

Regulators

The very heart of your diving support system is your regulator. The regulator takes high-pressure compressed air from a scuba tank and decreases the pressure through two stages until you're able to breathe it. Scuba regulators are what is known as demand regulators: Whenever you inhale, this triggers the regulator to deliver air.

These regulators are part of an open-circuit scuba system. *Open-circuit* means that as you exhale, the by-

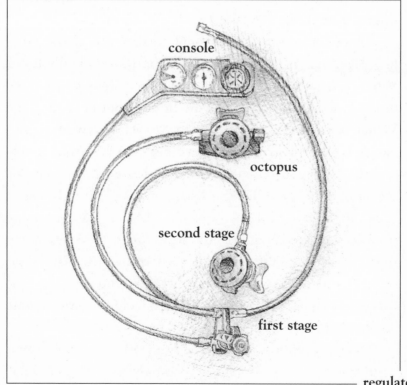

console

octopus

second stage

first stage

regulator

products of your respiration go into the water, not back into the system.

Closed-circuit systems, called rebreathers, are on the rise. They've been around for decades, used primarily by the military, but are now making their presence felt in recreational scuba. They are exactly what their name implies, closed (or partially closed) circuits in which the products of exhalation are fed back into the system, then cleaned and remixed for continued breathing. Some say that over the next five years, rebreathers may become a viable alternative to open-circuit scuba.

As a consumer, there are several things you need to know about regulators. The first is that there are no unsafe models on the market today. Any regulator that you can buy will work and is safe for the limits of recreational scuba. So what's the difference among all these regulators, other than the colored plastic inserts?

A major one is that all regulators breathe slightly differently. And this makes the selection process really hard. When you go in to buy a regulator, especially your first, it's kind of awkward to say, "Let me breathe out of each one." Which is, in fact, what you need to do. The irony of the situation is that as you improve as a diver, your breathing steadies out, and you develop a better sense of the type of regulator you would like. So I suggest postponing the regulator purchase for as long as possible. Use rental equipment from reputable companies. And each time you rent gear, try to get something different. Also, ask questions: What type of regulators does the store rent; what kind do the instructors own? That's the best way to get a feel for how different regulators breathe.

Some regulators are designed to work in more extreme conditions. They're also, not surprisingly, more expensive. If you plan to remain in recreational scuba, you don't need to consider these. They've been tested (by the military) at much deeper levels than a recreational diver is likely to encounter.

However, if you see your beginning dive experience as a preliminary step in a lifetime of diving—if you plan to move into different types of diving, maybe even into the technical diving realm—this will change the way you need to look at regulators. In fact, if you investigate the back of a diver's gear closet, you'll find that regulators and hoses tend to comprise a very substantial chunk of that obsolete, no-longer-used equipment.

Let me say up front that there are pieces of dive gear that you can cut costs on, but a regulator is not one of them. In fact, you want the very best regulator that you can afford. Again, there are no unsafe regulators on the market. But since you don't know where you're going with your scuba career—and especially if you think your scuba career may take you into technical or more extreme-type diving—it's better to start out with the regulator that you're going to need later than to have to buy a second system in six or eight months.

For the record, I'm still using the regulators that I purchased when I first started diving. They're made by Fee Systems in Florida. I've had no problems with them in recreational, cave, or deep wreck diving. Your goal, too, should be to buy equipment that you know is going to last you years and years.

First Stage

Sometimes it's a little daunting to look at regulators and see the listings that they carry of their features and functions. You may wonder, as I occasionally have, what half this stuff is, and which items have a direct effect on you as a beginning diver.

It may help you to know that regulators come in two stages. The first is the stage that attaches to the tank itself. The function of this stage is to take the first step toward reducing the pressure of the tank's air to something that you can breathe. Furthermore, there are two types of first stages—balanced and unbalanced. There aren't as many unbalanced first stages around these days as there used to be. Generally, an unbalanced first stage tends to be a little harder to breathe with under demand. There are exceptions to this statement, including at least one high-price regulator. Just recently, I made a business trip to the Bay Islands off Honduras. I wasn't planning on diving, but it seemed a shame to waste a week on Utila. The equipment I rented included a sturdy, well-maintained unbalanced system, and I experienced a definite difference between my breathing at 50 feet and my breathing at 100.

But again, this isn't much of an issue anymore; almost all first stages are fully balanced. The only unbalanced stages I know of that are widely in use are regulators on pony bottles (self-contained tanks of air a diver might carry as spares) and those used as rentals, due to simplicity and lower cost.

I also prefer first stages that are environmentally sealed—that is, not open to the water. One reason I like this is that I think the fewer corrosive elements contacting the working parts of the regulator, the better. Second, a sealed regulator works better in extreme conditions. As a recreational diver, you may never need a regulator that works in very cold water. But it's good to know that yours does.

However, I just talked to an experienced divemaster who feels exactly the opposite about sealing—and has 20 years of diving instruction to back him up.

A more important consideration in regulators is the type of connector. Every regulator has to be somehow connected to the tank valve. Most tanks use a yoke-type connector—a clamp-shaped arrangement. It goes over the top of the tank valve and has a yoke screw that tightens down, which provides the pressure needed to mate the regulator to the tank valve. Most regulators on the market are set up to work with yoke systems.

But lately there has been an influx of European-style DIN (Deutsches Institut fuer Normung) connectors. With a DIN connector, the regulator's first stage screws directly onto the tank valve. The DIN system offers a more secure arrangement: Your regulator is bolted to the tank. The system can also handle a higher pressure of air. And DIN systems eliminate one of the true irritations in scuba—that tiny rubber O-ring that has to fit on a yoke-system tank valve. That pesky O-ring is forever blowing out, because of bad karma or maybe the phase of the moon. I'm always finding O-rings stuck in my shorts pockets, lying around my desk, everywhere but where I really need them, which is on the tank valve. With a DIN system, though, the O-ring is captive. The little beggar can't get away.

I would suggest doing what I did, which is get a regulator setup with a DIN fitting and an optional yoke adapter, so that you can use your system with any tank. (My personal tanks are obviously set up for DIN, and I've never had any problem with the adapter.) This setup gives you the best the both worlds. If you're traveling a lot, on cattle boats or down in the Caribbean, you're likely to see yokes. If you have a chance to use DIN, do so. If not, you've got the yoke adaptor. So go for this versatility—and remember to carry O-rings!

Most regulators now have plenty of accessory ports for hooking up various devices needing air. I like first-stage regulators that have the low-pressure ports arranged on some kind of swivel, so I have some options in how I set up my tank-and-regulator system.

Typically, in single-tank recreational scuba you'll have your low-pressure hose coming in over your left shoulder. And that feeds to the second-stage regulator in your mouth.

Second Stage

There're substantially fewer options with the second stage. In fact, usually your only choices are matters of style: whether your exhaled breath is going to go out the side or the bottom of the regulator; the type of regulator valve; and, finally, the level of adjustment of that valve.

You're almost certainly going to be buying the first and second stages as a package. As you progress in your diving, mix-and-match becomes more of an option.

Most regulators are what's called downstream—the valve opens away from the air flow. When you inhale, a diaphragm presses against the demand level, which is directly connected to a one-way valve. The valve opens; you get air.

Such downstream models are simple and cost less than the alternative. One of their advantages is if the regulator fails by locking open, air will continue to come out and you can continue to breathe, though you'll exhaust the air supply at a much quicker rate.

The other type of regulator is called the pilot valve. It basically provides a little greater air flow with less effort. The downside is if the regulator itself fails, it shuts off your air.

Again, in selecting your regulator, breathe it. Don't purchase a regulator without testing it. The best way to do this is through either a demo program at your dive shop or equipment rentals.

Just as an aside, you'll also be purchasing an alternate air source, the simplest of which is called an octopus. It's a second regulator. There's a tendency, which I have never really understood, to purchase a lesser-quality regulator as a secondary air source. But the functions of this backup are to enable you to breathe should your primary regulator cease functioning, and to help your partner should he or she run out of air or experience primary and secondary air source failures. Thus I want my secondary air source to be exactly the same regulator as my primary air source. Because, first, I'm pretty sure my buddy is every bit as important as I am. And, second, if my primary regulator fails for some reason, the secondary becomes the primary.

I generally don't like alternate air source-BCD inflator combinations—the kind where the secondary regulator is attached to the hose that serves to inflate a buoyancy control device. The system works, but you have less hose to deal with, which means a bit less versatility. Still, an alternate air source inflator can serve as yet another piece of redundancy equipment—a tertiary regulator, of sorts. If your first and second regulators fail, you have yet another fallback.

8:

Instrumentation, Buoyancy, and Keeping Warm

ou're going to need a good bit of information down there. The data that you absolutely must have at your fingertips are *cylinder pressure*—how much air you actually have left to breathe—*depth,* and *time.* The latter two, of course, because you'll need to make sure you're following your dive plan and stay within the no-decompression limits.

There are a lot of different ways to get this information—the array of instruments is daunting. As a new diver, you're going to get the first piece of information, cylinder pressure, from the submersible pressure gauge attached to your tank. The other information will most likely come from a dive computer.

Computers

Since their introduction more than a decade ago, dive computers have revolutionized the sport. The main reason for this is that computers can constantly refigure your bottom time based on "real world" depth data.

All divers learn to figure bottom times using dive tables—basically charts used to gauge how much residual nitrogen you have in your body, allowing you to determine safe time and depth limits. Most are based on U.S. Navy dive tables, which were originally put together for navy hardhat divers.

Dive computers are, at their most basic, computerized versions of these tables. When you figure dives using tables, however, you get what is referred to as a square dive profile: You descend, have bottom time, and ascend. Chart this and you have a square. Multilevel dives are figured as multiple square profiles.

But a square profile generally doesn't reflect the reality of diving. It's based on your maximum depth, but in actuality you may spend only a small portion of your dive at the deepest point. A quick example—last week I made a reef dive, and I figured a dive profile at 85 feet. Based on the U.S. Navy dive table, that gave me 30 minutes of bottom time. (And that's the most liberal table—the one that allows the most bottom time. Some of the other dive tables I have list the bottom time for 90 feet—rounding up, as always—as from 22 to 25 minutes.) On the actual dive, however, I spent four minutes at the deepest point, 85 feet. The bulk of my time was spent at around 60 feet, with a long portion at 45.

Because a computer chip has tons of figuring capacity, however, it can constantly refigure my remaining bottom time based not on a square profile, but on my real-life profile. By following my computer, I was able to lengthen my dive—including a safety stop at 15 feet—to around 41 minutes.

In your first open water training, you were probably introduced to the computer as an upgrade to the more basic instruments of a depth gauge and a timer. In the last two years, however, the price of computers has dropped so low that they're pretty much ubiquitous. Some of the big Caribbean resorts offer computers as part of their rental packages, or, at the least, allow experienced computer users to follow different dive profiles than people working off tables must.

I consider a dive computer a piece of essential equipment. You're going to end up with one anyway, and I've found it takes several—sometimes many—dives to get a feel for the amount of information displayed on the screen. So the sooner you start getting used to the specific brand of computer you choose, the better.

Computers are one of those items that *can* be comparison-shopped, because—as with regulators—there are no bad ones on the market at this point. A couple of years ago, that was not the case; there were some real dogs out there. But right now, most computers are good, and any of the name-brand computers will do a good job.

Make sure the computer you purchase allows for staged decompression diving—some of the older ones didn't. If you continue in your diving career, you're likely to encounter a situation where you must make stops at specific levels as you ascend to allow the accumulated nitrogen to bleed out of your tissues. In this case, you'll want a computer that figures the depth of each stop and the time you need to spend there. For your recreational diving, though, think of this feature as an added safety factor.

Eventually, you may even reach the limits of your computer. As scuba becomes more sophisticated, the current batch of computers will run up against their limitations. For example, I made a technical dive recently to below 200 feet. The dive involved breathing trimix on the bottom, followed by a long staged decompression that included two different mixes of enriched air—nitrox 32 (32% oxygen) and 36 (36% oxygen)—and, finally, pure oxygen at the shallowest decompression stop. My computers, all programmed based on compressed-air times, would have had strokes trying to figure those times. There are some excellent nitrox and mixed-gas computers, but more often than not a complex dive requires depth gauges and timers.

Typically, for recreational scuba, you'll mount your computer in your instrument console—that collection of gauges usually attached to the first stage of the regulator to accommodate the tank-pressure gauge. The hose for the console usually comes over your shoulder. Rather than having my console swinging all over the place, I bungee it to a D-ring on my BCD. The newest high-tech, high-trick systems integrate the tank-pressure function into the computer. But generally, your air isn't integrated into your computer functions.

As an option, you can mount your computer on a wristband. For recreational diving, or if I'm using only one computer, I like a console-mounted model. Sometimes a wrist-mounted computer is a little bit harder to deal with—there are a couple of irritations. You have to put the computer on after you put on your exposure suit, for one, and on a rocking, wet dive boat when you're truly seasick, even putting on the computer is a major challenge.

It can also get lost. My friend Bill Belleville lost $600 worth of computer into a blue hole in the Bahamas because he snagged his wristband on a rock. A sharp piece of coral simply cut through the band, and the computer fell into the abyss.

I have both systems. On a normal dive, I use two computers: the wrist-mounted computer as my primary and the console-mounted unit as a secondary.

Often when I'm on a business trip to the coast or out of the country, I take along my mask and wrist-mounted computer in the hope of getting in a dive or two. Aside from the huge advantage of having data I trust, my computer has a log function (as do most computers), so I can review my dives when I get home in a vain attempt to keep my logbook current. In your open water class you were given your first logbook and told about how important it was to keep it current. You probably religiously logged your first few dives. That religion has a way of waning. As a friend of mine, a writer for *Outside* magazine and a veteran diver, once told me, "You mean people actually have logbooks? You're not joking with me, are you?" About two years ago, after I had to whine, bitch, and moan my way onto a dive trip because I couldn't produce a logbook showing five dives below 150 feet, I bought one and began keeping records. Or, actually, the computer began keeping records, and I began transcribing them into the book.

Computers, by the way, don't necessarily all agree, just as not all dive tables agree. Some computers are more liberal—allowing more bottom time—than others, because their makers use different formulas for calculating residual nitrogen. All computer makers have extensive documentation to back up their algorithms, though.

Of my two computers, the wrist unit is the more conservative. And that's why I tend to follow it, with the second computer acting as a backup. I have trained myself, then, to check the wrist computer, then the console, for the remaining air.

Look at the different types of computers and the information they make available to you. Check how easy it is to access that information. Remember that the primary data you need are your depth, time, remaining air, and maximum bottom time. You want that information at your fingertips at all times.

Do a little comparison shopping. Dive computers are aggressively and competitively marketed. And don't forget to use your retail shop intelligence network.

Buoyancy Control Devices

BCDs are inflation vests that help you achieve neutral buoyancy in the water. There are a lot of them out there, and you need to find one that fits you well. Actually, I've found that the more I dive, the less that elusive fit seems to matter. They all seem to fit okay, from the nattiest, most ultramodern units to the ones that look like they've been gnawed by rats and stored in the bottom of the closet for a decade. As long as they inflate and deflate, I pretty much don't care.

There are two major kinds of BCDs: the buoyancy control jacket, certainly the most common, and a simple back-mounted bladder usually called "wings." If you keep diving, you'll probably end up with wings. For now, though, think jacket. What you're looking for here is fit—or, rather, a bad fit. If you just hate the thing, pass on it no matter what the price. Most BCDs work extremely well, so if you can find a good fit at a lower price, go ahead and save some money.

One of the things I really like about buoyancy control devices these days is D-rings, those stainless-steel rings that allow you to clip things to your vest. I like to have a number of them so I can hang an extra light, an extra knife, stage bottles, whatever. I much prefer D-rings to extra pockets, which are fiercely hard to manipulate under water even under the best conditions—and when you need to reach your backup gear, it's usually not because you're in the best conditions. But D-rings keep all my necessary gear in the same place and easily accessible.

Lead weights are attached to your body to enable you to sink. Those weights can either go on a separate belt or in a pocket. I prefer integrated weight pockets; a belt just gives me one more thing to worry about.

Suits

Over the years, I've been involved in many sports that require some sort of exposure suit, whether a skin suit, a wet suit, or a dry suit. As a result, I own lots of wet suits in various stages of decomposition. From this I've evolved Michael's Inescapable Law of Wet Suits: "Salt water and ultraviolet radiation always win." I've come to view wet suits as consumables. Take care of them as best you can, but in the end salt, sunshine, water pressure, and the endless abrasions of entering and exiting the water take their toll. This is why most experienced divers you see are wearing wet suits that give them the appearance of ragamuffins. Want to save some money? Save it here. I have a heavy wet suit for cold-water diving, which I bought on a 66 percent off clearance sale at a local dive shop. It replaced my last clearance-sale wet suit. I also have an excellent hood-vest combo for additional warmth and a bunch of different gloves. My wet suit will never be featured in a James Bond film, but it'll do the job.

Wet suits keep you warm by means of a thin layer of water, heated by your body, between the suit and your skin. Dry suits are different beasts entirely. A dry suit seals out the water and keeps a layer of warm air between the suit and your skin. Wear nice fleece undies with your dry suit and you can be warm under the polar cap. You can also buy a used car with what you'll spend for a dry suit. When you get to the point that you need one, you'll know. Then you can start the discussion on how much of the kids' college fund you're going to loot. Dry suits also require special training, so plan on taking a class. I meticulously maintain my dry suit, including lubricating the seals with whatever bizarre synthetic oils the manufacturer recommends.

Equipment Strategizing for Travel

What I carry on a dive trip depends on where I'm going and the nature of the diving I'll be doing. As I mentioned earlier, on a recent trip to Central America, where diving wasn't my main activity, I carried only my mask, my primary dive computer, and a set of tables. The area was known for its diving and had numerous dive shops, so I was certain that equipment rental would hardly be a problem. I was right. For a very few bucks, I was able to rent brand-new gear exactly like what I had at home.

On the other hand, my partner Bill "Where Did My Computer Go?" Belleville and I are planning a cave diving trip to the north shore of Cuba. We'll be carrying tons of equipment—everything we can think of, and spares, right down to our own tanks. We've been assured by our Cuban contacts that tanks are available, but neither one of us is willing to risk getting low-quality or poorly maintained equipment.

Your dive trips will probably fall between those two extremes; most likely you'll be heading to recreational dive destinations. I've traveled around the world for various sports and find that the older I get, the less I want to carry. If I was going to Grand Cayman for a 10-day dive vacation,

for example, I would carry mask, regulators and console, computers and tables. Maybe my fins. I would not carry a BCD, tanks, or exposure suit, because I know I can rent what I need when I get there. More expensive? Excess luggage valuation is $45 each way.

I also don't like to travel with huge bags that proudly proclaim, "Really expensive gear inside!" Instead, I use cheap, military surplus parachute bags for most of my gear, and always carry on my mask and instrumentation.

9:

Beyond
the
First
C-Card

You finally finished all your instruction for the basic dive course, Open Water I. You've actually passed the tests. You've learned the basics of safety, equipment rigging, and figuring bottom times for single and multiple dives; you've touched on the basics of the undersea environment. You've completed your training dives and been able to demonstrate the fundamental skills of scuba—you can flood and clear your mask, you can buddy-breathe, you can ascend at a slow, steady rate. You've gotten that coveted C-card, a picture ID that allows you to get your tanks filled with air whenever and wherever you want.

So what should you do next? There are two schools of thought. One is that you should just dive for a while. Try to get in a lot of basic dives and get a feel for the underwater environment and what you want to do.

The second school of thought is that you should sign up for more instruction. In Open Water I (or the equivalent), you were also introduced to the higher levels of instruction—advanced open water, specialty courses, nitrox, and, beyond that, technical diving courses. You're probably shaking your head at this point, thinking, "Aha, of course they want me to sign up for more instruction. That's what they get paid for. This guy is a shill for the scuba industry!"

When I first got my C-card, my instructors were of the opinion that I needed to take a year to dive, spend time looking at the underwater environment, and try to get in, say, 20 dives before I took the next level of classes. At the time I lived in Florida, so that wasn't difficult to do. However, even if you have the time and money to dive before you move onto more instruction, is it the wisest course?

I don't think so, and let me tell you why. You've spent a lot of time, money, and effort to get that first certification card. In many ways, that first C-card is like the learner's driving permit you got when you were 15. You didn't actually think, back then, that you were going immediately to Indianapolis to do a couple of quick laps on the track. What you thought—if you had any sense, which some of us lacked—was that you finally had a chance to spend a little time in the car and learn how the thing worked.

Unfortunately, unlike the learner's permit, the C-card doesn't require you to have a more experienced diver along. Most of us got into diving through a friend or spouse or some person close to us who was a diver. The drawback to this, though, is that you end up with an imbalance of technical skills between you and your dive pal.

There's an old song that says something to the effect that spouses should never ever attempt to teach each other. That it's the best way to guarantee those spouses cease to be spousal units. There's a lot to that.

I've met many women who took dive lessons, then stopped diving because the pressure from their husbands created situations in which they were uncomfortable.

One reason scuba diving appeals so much to men is that it's such a gadget-driven sport. It's not unusual to find men—and sometimes women—who have given themselves totally over to scuba-gadget lust. And when that happens, it puts pressure on the nontechnical member of the pair.

An imbalance develops. One partner wants to push limits, while the less advanced partner is trying to feel comfortable at a much different level.

I was in this situation myself. I began by diving with people who were far more experienced than I, and far more capable. As a new diver with a basic C-card, I didn't know my limits, and therefore I couldn't begin testing them.

The first few dives that you take after getting your C-card have the potential of being one of two things: either the very best dives you've ever had, dives that really open your eyes to scuba and the underwater environment; or some of the most terrifying experiences in your life.

Up until the point that you're on your own, or with a spouse or friend or group of friends, you had an instructor who told you what to do. He or she pointed out the danger areas, checked your equipment, and planned your dive. You felt secure. But now all of a sudden you're out there on your own, or with others who may or may not be more experienced than you are. Let me tell you, it can be petrifying.

There are a lot of divers who complete two or three dives on their own, then never dive again. They found the experience too stressful and frightening. Their fears weren't present in the more supervised setting of instruction, and they were never able to get beyond those fears.

The best way to make sure that this doesn't happen to you is to sign up immediately for a second tier of courses. Almost all the dive certifying agencies offer the next level. That might be Advanced Open Water or Open Water II. It's more of the same. You won't learn huge amounts of new material, but you will refine your existing knowledge base.

People who immediately sign up for the next level of classes are more likely to stay in scuba. When they begin diving on their own, they're more likely to be more comfortable, because they have more supervised dives under their belts. Also, they know more about the underwater environment and, consequently, are more comfortable in it.

The other thing that second-tier dive training provides is an introduction to the specialties. These include underwater navigation, night diving, drift diving, diving from a boat, deep diving, dry suit diving, multilevel diving, search and recover diving, underwater photography, underwater naturalism, wreck diving, research diving, hunting and spearfishing, ice diving, and cavern diving. Each of these specialties—still within the realm of recreational diving—offers you a way of expanding on the basics.

More than that, each of the specialties, which all require their own certification process, represents a niche in the diving world. Each also exposes you to conditions that, as an advanced open water diver, you may well come across. For example, night diving teaches some critical skills, because in your diving career you're very likely to encounter limited visibility, which is tremendously stressful. But in night diving classes, you learn how to function in limited visibility, so it'll be that much easier to do so when that situation presents itself in the real world.

It's not unusual to find divers who "collect" specialties, sort of like collecting merit badges when you were a Boy or Girl Scout. You get to add another patch to your jacket at the same time you're making yourself a better, more well-rounded diver.

I once read an article in a foreign magazine about a doctor who had survived the crash of two jumbo jets in the Canary Islands years ago. The doctor explained that the reason he had survived the crash, while many others had been killed, was that he adopted what he called his "index card theory of life." The brain, he said, is like a big box that stores index cards.

Whenever there's a crisis, whenever you enter a situation that's scary enough to trigger the old fight-or-flight response, your brain sorts through its index cards. Each is a response to a certain stimuli: *If this happens, I should do that . . . if I see a saber-toothed tiger licking its lips, I should run like crazy.*

If the brain can't find the index card for a specific crisis, it makes a call to its thinking section and says, "Okay, now what?" But a life-threatening situation is not the best time for the back part of your brain to call and say it doesn't know what to do.

So you need that index card for every potential crisis. That's what the doctor in the article had. As soon as he sat down on the plane he looked around for the exit and said to himself, "Should something happen to the plane on the ground, I'm going to grab my wife, jump to the right, jerk open the door, and get out of the plane."

In other words, he created a mental index card that gave him a specific set of actions to perform should a specific situation take place. As it happened, two planes collided on the ground. The doctor jumped up, grabbed his wife, leaped to the right, ripped open the door, slid out on the wing, and escaped the fire. He was then able to go back and help rescue other people. He didn't have to think—that's the key. He responded automatically to an index card that he had prepared earlier.

Advanced dive training offers many opportunities to create similar index cards for "what if" situations.

When I encounter a less-than-optimum situation on a dive, then, I already have a response. If you and your spouse, friend, or partner go through the same training, you'll have the same prepared response.

Two specialties that will make you a better diver are underwater navigation and the aforementioned night diving.

Underwater Navigation

In underwater navigation class you'll learn to use a

compass to navigate under water. Just as important and sometimes overlooked is that the course will teach you to locate references under water, enabling you to find your way around. Naturally, as you're diving you take note of what you see: "There's a clump of coral, there's a funny rock formation, there's the way that the reef line runs." Still, underwater navigation training teaches you to think about those points not just as interesting items under water, but also as ways for you to find your way home. It teaches you the important skill of being observant.

Thus it's also a good way to alleviate stress in new divers. If you can find your way home, or back to that down line or anchor line, you're going to be a lot more comfortable than you would be if you questioned where home was.

Additionally, a specialty in underwater navigation provides the groundwork for future, more technical, dive training.

The first few times you dive on your own—you may have already noticed this in your classes—you're often so overwhelmed by the experience of being under water and by the necessity of working with your equipment that, next thing you know, it's time to go up and you haven't had a chance to look around.

Or you may find that while you do see things, it's hard to remember them. If you're ever along on an early certifying dive with a large class, ask them what they saw as they surface. Generally, they don't see nearly as much as you'd expect. It's simply because their senses were overwhelmed.

But when you're in an underwater environment, the need for very clear observations increases: You need to be aware of everything going on around you.

Often divers report fish sneaking up on them. Of all the things that fish do, sneaking up on people is, I suspect, a fairly low priority. Generally, the divers just didn't notice the fish until it was right on top of them. (Barracudas are especially good at this.)

One method I've found helpful in increasing my observation is something that I borrowed from police SWAT teams and special military units. When you're moving in an alien environment, such as under water, you should heighten your level of alertness.

These special teams often rate their level of awareness by means of colors: white, green, yellow, and red. A white level means you're totally unaware of what is going on around you. Green means you're in a relaxed state of awareness. You're paying attention, but there's nothing that sends up an alarm. Yellow means something about the environment has pricked your senses. You're suddenly paying a bit more attention in that area. A red level is a response to a critical situation. You must be on full alert.

So what color should you be in while diving?

I'd say green. Relaxed awareness of your environment at all times. You should never be in white while you're diving. On your very first dives, you're stuck in classic white mode, because there is so much new information and gear, in such a strange environment, that it's all you can do to continue breathing and keep from bouncing off the bottom. Don't stay at this white level, though.

What I like about this color system of alertness is that it allows me to visualize raising my level of alertness—without raising it too fast. For new divers, I've often observed that alertness comes in only two flavors: *I'm not aware of anything,* and *Oh my God, it's going to eat me!*

If you think in terms of a color continuum, though, you can see that when you spy something out of the ordinary, something slightly strange, your level of awareness should move from green to yellow. You should pay attention to the anomaly in the environment without going to red alert.

How to stay in green mode is one of the things that underwater navigation class helps you learn. It teaches you to keep looking: ahead, to your sides, behind. It teaches you to focus in on landmarks that allow you to navigate. Once you have this level of awareness you can anticipate the potential changes in your environment, and you can prepare to compensate for them. Remember, make index cards.

For example, is the current picking up? Is the water temperature changing? Have you dropped below a thermocline level (a level at which water temperature changes radically)? Is there anything around that may pose a threat to yourself or your equipment? If you're near a wreck, do you see any jagged pieces of metal to avoid? In open water, is there a lot of sharp coral, or fire coral?

Fighter pilots make preliminary checks before they go up in their airplanes. In the air, they constantly scan the skies and instruments. Not because they're worried, not because they're frightened, but because they want the earliest possible notice when the situation changes.

In diving, your mask shaves away a portion of your peripheral vision. Consequently, things can go on behind you, or at the extreme limits of your peripheral vision, that can take you by surprise. You need to train yourself to keep checking within a 360-degree field. Also, be aware of where your buddy is at all times, and what he or she is doing. If you're diving with a group, know where it is and what the members are doing. If you're with a guide, know where the guide is going.

At the same time you're looking around in a 360-degree field, and keeping track of your dive partners, you must process all this information in such a way that you can find your way home. Your goal is to be able to look back and see a trail of specific reference points, so that you're not only aware of what's going on around you, but also aware of where you are within the underwater space.

Night Diving

There are a lot of reasons to night-dive, including the one I mentioned earlier: It's a good way to prepare yourself for limited visibility. The underwater world becomes very different when the sun goes down, too; the night dwellers come out and it's a haunting, almost hypnotic place.

Night diving also gives you a chance to practice the navigation skills you learned in your underwater navigation course. A compass is required on a night dive. Otherwise, how will you know where you're going? You can't necessarily see landmarks.

Night diving also gives you a really good introduction to task loading. (See chapter 11 for more on this.) Adding tasks to a dive induces stress, and even more so in the dark. Things that are simple during the day become more complicated at night—keeping track of your buddy, remaining aware of the environment around you, even handling equipment.

So what are some of the things night diving teaches? First is the importance of planning. If you've planned your dive well, your equipment well, and the people you're diving with well, it's going to make for a much easier dive. That's a lesson you can take back to any other type of diving.

Second, you're going to reacquaint yourself with your friend Mr. Redundancy.

Obviously, on a night dive you need a light. This means you'll actually need two lights: a primary light, and a secondary, or backup, light.

Since you just got through paying big bucks for the primary light, why do you need the secondary? Well, basically because all things fail. And if you're diving in salt water, know that salt water always wins.

On a typical night dive I like to carry a primary light, which is generally handheld, and a secondary, which I like to put in a jacket pocket attached to a D-ring on my BCD. I prefer a smaller flashlight as a backup. It will fit within a pocket but still provide me with the light I need for ascent or if anything should happen to my primary.

I've tried a lot of different types of lights, including the natty little headlights that clip onto your mask. I like these because they make it easy to check my equipment; wherever I look, there's a little light. The drawbacks are that I've never had a headlight that didn't fail very quickly, and that my buddy gets tired of me blinding him every time I look at him. Once, a buddy gave me the universal underwater signal for "I'm going to kill you and leave your body for the fish"—two hands around the throat.

Night diving also helps the beginning diver cope with the concept of disorientation. When you're diving in daylight you know which way is up. You can always see your bubbles, and your bubbles always go up. At night, with those telltale bubbles invisible, it's easy to become disoriented. Shine your light on them—they still go up, even in the dark.

Wreck Diving

Other than watching the flora and fauna under water, wrecks may be the greatest single attraction for divers.

They're one of those things that you either get or don't get. I've known divers who went down to a wreck and returned to say, "Gee, that's kind of like visiting an automobile junkyard at the bottom of the ocean."

Other divers I know were totally hooked after their first wreck.

I once spent some time with the New York City-New Jersey wreckers, a whole crew of divers whose lives center on diving deep wrecks, of which there are many in the Northeast. And they are truly obsessive. When diving, they seem to be actually wearing a junkyard, as opposed to just visiting one. They've got chisels, they've got wrenches. In one case, we dove with an air-powered impact hammer for chipping away pieces of wrecks. Their homes are filled with little pieces of shipwrecks.

But that very first wreck dive, the one you'll make while training for your advanced card, is going to help you work within yet another aspect of the underwater environment.

Wrecks are a lot less forgiving than open water. There's jagged metal and many ways to get tangled up. You won't initially go in the wreck, but you'll swim around it and look inside. When you feel comfortable around wrecks, you'll feel even more comfortable in open water.

Deep Diving

Getting your first exposure to deep diving as part of your advanced training is particularly important. Unfortunately, most divers get their introduction to it on their own, usually about their third or fourth dive. You'd be amazed at the number of divers who actually brag about how deep they went within their first five dives. One recently told me, "You know, I got to 170 feet on my fourth dive."

That's not a good idea. The reason is that the deeper you go—and this will be covered in more detail in chapter 11—the less margin for error you have.

PADI, my first certifying agency, defines a *deep dive* as "any dive deeper than 60 feet." Your first C-card certifies you to dive down to 60 feet in the conditions under which you were trained. And these vary wildly. I was trained in Florida, and my certification dives came both in the Keys and in Maui. Warm water, lots of sunlight, super visibility. Big difference between this and where my friend David Feeney conducts his open water certifications, which is off one of the piers in Brooklyn. There, the visibility is zero, there are heavy currents, and it's cold. It's really scary. So where you were trained affects what you are certified to do.

When you move into advanced open water courses, you'll be able to get down to between 100 and 130 feet. That latter figure is widely considered to be the limit of recreational scuba diving.

However, this limit is the single most abused among new divers. When the guy told me he'd hit 170 feet on his fourth dive, I took him to task. What would his responses have been if something had gone wrong? What if his equipment had failed, or he'd stayed too long and had to come to the surface in a staged decompression dive? His response was, "Hey, as long as nothing goes wrong, there's no problem."

Well, that's a little bit like saying that as long as nothing goes wrong in skydiving, there's no problem. It reminds me of a quote attributed to Amelia Earhart: Air travel per se is safe; it's only when the plane comes in contact with the ground that there're problems.

Remember subjective and objective risks. In deep diving, both the subjective and the objective risk factors get bigger and bigger and bigger. There's more in the environment that can hurt you, and there's less margin for error. The deeper you get, the less you are able to get away with things that were no problem in shallower dives.

So one of the great benefits conferred by an advanced open water class is a little more respect for depth.

I've actually been puzzled over why people want to go deeper and deeper, even though every instructor I have ever met has cautioned students against it.

I think the problem is that in scuba, unlike other risk sports, you can't necessarily see the risks. If you're going to climb a 10-foot-high wall without a rope, you know that, realistically, if you fall you might sprain or break your ankle and it might hurt. One look at that wall can give you a sense of the real risks involved in climbing it.

If you took that same wall and put it at the top of a telephone pole, everything would change. You'd look at it and realize that if you fell, you'd probably die.

Likewise, a mountaineer can look at a climb and objectively see its risks. Obviously, an experienced climber can do that a lot more precisely than a nonclimber. But it just makes sense—the higher up you go, the more force you're going to hit the ground with, and the greater the risk you're taking. In mountaineering, that's called exposure.

If you then climb the cliff face, you'll get constant sensory and psychological feedback telling you you're outside of your comfort zone. After all, we're an arboreal species—so they tell us. And for a species that evolved in the trees, the great universal fear is falling. So there on the cliff all your senses will tell you, "Watch out; danger." The higher you climb, the louder the messages, even if you're roped in.

Diving is just the opposite. And it's dark; you can't see. So you can go deeper and deeper without your senses ever telling you, "Wow, this is a lot more dangerous, pay attention, pay attention." There's no innate warning, as there is against falling. And, in fact, the deeper you go, the more likely you are to experience nitrogen narcosis (covered in more detail in chapter 12): Some of its effects are going to blunt your stimulus response. The classic line holds that if you're below 100 feet and you feel comfortable and safe, you're "narked," because you *shouldn't* feel comfortable and safe there.

Deep diving classes, along with the first level of technical training, deep air diving (as opposed to using breathing mixes other than air), help teach proper respect for the deep realms.

10:

Thinking about Decompression

In your basic open water classes you learned that as you go deeper, the nitrogen in the compressed air that you're breathing is forced into your tissues.

This is because the body seeks an equilibrium. At the surface, that equilibrium is achieved. The gases in your lungs are balanced out by the gases in your tissues. But because of nitrogen's higher partial pressures, as you descend it gets stored as a dissolved gas throughout your body tissues.

That stored gas must be out-gassed from the tissues as you return to the surface. Otherwise, you run the risk of decompression sickness (DCS)—or decompression illness (DSI)—which results from the formation of nitrogen bubbles within your tissues. These bubbles can cause tremendous damage to the body, sometimes even disability or death. Things are a little vague as to the "whys" of DCS. While it's accepted that the nitrogen bubbles in the blood are the root of the problem, physiologists do not yet understand the exact mechanism by which the bubbles harm the body.

There are factors that can predispose you to DCS, including fat, dehydration, advancing age, alcohol, cold water, and heavy exercise. DCS is usually categorized as Type I, involving only skin and pain manifestations, and Type II, which includes all central nervous system manifestations. And those manifestations are many—ranging from a Type I skin rash to joint and limb pain, and damage to the central nervous system, which might simply impair functions such as touch, or might involve paralysis or even death. Bubbles can also reach the brain, where they can cause blurred vision, headaches, confusion, unconsciousness, stroke, and, again, death. If the bubbles make it to the lungs, they can block the flow of blood through that organ, which leads to a choking cough and a shutdown of the circulatory system. The bubbles can also leave a trail of havoc through other parts of the body—though this is rare. All in all, DCS is something you want to avoid.

And decompression—the controlled removal of excess nitrogen from the body during ascent—is the way to avoid it.

How do you provide that control? In your first open water class you learned to work with two key tools—dive tables and computers. Both gauge how much excess nitrogen you have in your body. This lets you determine the maximum amount of time you can spend at a certain depth, and also the way you have to ascend to guarantee the removal of that stored nitrogen from your tissues. (Flip back to chapter 8 for a complete discussion of these tools.) I use tables distributed by the International Association of Nitrox and Technical Divers, for reasons I'll explain later.

Now, the question is, does the use of computers and dive tables guarantee that you'll never get decompression sickness?

No. The study of decompression sickness is, at best, an inexact science. It's been going on a long time. In fact, the very first work on decompression sickness was done by J. B. S. Haldane in England in 1908. He studied DCS not among divers, but among bridge and pier workers laboring deep underground in caissons.

The workers who had the misfortune of being struck by DCS tended to walk with a stoop—those who could still walk—which was similar to the posture affected by the society ladies at the time and known as the Grecian Bend. So their comrades would make fun of the stricken workers by saying that they had the "bends." That word, of course, has stuck with us a heck of a lot longer than the fashionable Grecian Bend.

There are two ways that stored nitrogen is eliminated from the body. The first is the very basic one you learned in your open water class: As you start ascending, the pressure around you decreases, and the nitrogen that has been absorbed into your tissues begins to leave them. Breathe slowly and ascend slowly, and the excess nitrogen will be steadily eliminated.

The second method for controlling the removal of nitrogen from the body is one that has been around since the very beginning of diving. It's called staged decompression, and it involves ascending to a certain point (precalculated through either the tables or a computer) and staying there for a predetermined amount of time to allow the nitrogen to bleed out of the tissues. After you've been at the decompression point for the specified amount of time, you move up to a shallower decompression point and, again, remain there for a predetermined amount of time.

In your basic classes, you learned to make a "safety stop": a three-minute rest at 15 feet. This safety stop, is, in fact, a decompression stop.

There's a tendency among beginners to think there are two different kinds of diving: one within the no-stop limits taught in Open Water I, and another that requires staged decompression stops.

In fact, though, there's only one type. All diving is decompression diving. As soon as you head downward in the water, your body begins seeking equilibrium, and its tissues begin absorbing excess nitrogen. Ascend, and the nitrogen is out-gassed. There are simply two different strategies for dealing with that excess nitrogen. However, the no-stop method is only effective for dives with a limited amount of bottom time and depth.

Staged Decompression

Sooner or later, you're going to exceed your no-stop limits. You'll exceed the bottom time provided by your dive table for ascending directly to the surface.

You should have already been taught a procedure for dealing with this. Briefly, though, if you accidentally exceed a no-decompression limit by less than five minutes, ascend to your 15-foot stop and stay there for eight minutes. And don't dive again for six hours.

The procedure for exceeding the no-stop limit by more than five minutes is slowly ascending to the 15-foot stop, staying there for 15 minutes—air supply permitting—and then discontinuing diving for the rest of the day.

If you've already been thinking about these procedures, you've already been filling out the appropriate mental index cards for potential problems.

A couple of years ago, I asked many of my diver friends about their first staged decompression dive. Was it planned, or did it just happen by accident?

Almost unanimously, that first staged decompression dive had been an accident. Then, through a series of hits and misses, everybody had gotten used to dealing with staged decompression (or, simply, decompression) diving.

My first decompression dive was out in the Atlantic, on a wreck 90 feet down—not particularly deep. It wasn't entirely an accident; I had the idea in the back of my mind that it wasn't going to be a big deal. I was carrying extra air, so I planned to stay down a little longer. I thought (far too casually) that I'd stop when my computer told me to. Which is exactly what I did. Then I ran out of air at the 15-foot stop, with three minutes remaining.

So I ascended to the surface and sat around the boat and worried for the next two or three hours over whether I was going to get some of the symptoms of DCS. I was lucky—no hits.

That most first staged decompression dives happen by accident goes against one of the basic precepts of dive training, which is that you don't want any surprises. You don't want something to happen that causes your brain to open up the index card file, flip through it, and say, "Wow, there's no index card for this! What am I going to do?"

The problem is that staged decompression diving falls into a big crack between recreational scuba and the newer fields of technical diving. So you can go through advanced training and specialty training without learning about it.

When it came up in my Open Water I class, the way it was addressed was simply, "Don't put yourself in that sort of situation, intentionally or unintentionally."

Technical classes in deep air diving do deal with it, but tend to assume that you already know the basics of and have some experience in staged decompression diving.

So everyone does it, but nobody really talks about it. You end up learning it from books, and perfecting it through trial and error. I don't think that's the way to do it.

Before going any farther, I'd like to strongly recommend that you don't do any staged decompression diving until you've been thoroughly trained and signed lots of liability releases. Nothing in the following description should be construed as suggesting you should do a staged decompression dive at this point, as I heartily advise against it.

That said, you should still *think* about what might happen, or what set of circumstances might exist, that would cause you, however ill-advisedly, to get into a staged decompression situation. Wreck diving, for example, could put you at risk, especially to the 100- to 110-foot depth.

Why is this? Generally, you paid a lot of money to get there. At 110 feet you've got about 15 or 16 minutes of bottom time. With a wreck, it often takes 15 or 16 minutes simply to get a feel for it. You're just starting to be able to look around. You're peering into nooks and crannies, seeing lots of really fascinating ocean life. Uh-oh . . . look at the time!

So if you think there's a chance you may end up in a situation where you have to do a staged decompression, what sorts of index cards can you put into place to eliminate your doing something stupid and dangerous, like making an emergency ascent from 15 feet because you ran out of air?

This is where your dive buddy comes in. I've mentioned this concept off and on throughout this book. You are taught in recreational scuba, no matter what the certifying agency, the importance of a dive buddy. You communicate with that dive buddy. The dive buddy checks you out before the dive. The dive buddy is there in case you run out of air. You can make an emergency ascent while breathing off your dive buddy's octopus. It is the safest way of diving.

However, there's one thing your dive buddy cannot do for you: think.

New recreational divers sometimes see their dive buddy as a crutch—"If I do something really wrong, this guy's here to save me."

That's simply not the case. Yes, a buddy team is the safest way to dive. But you can never abdicate your own responsibility for your personal safety to another person.

It's not fair to the other person. It's not inconceivable to find yourself in a situation in which you put your buddy at risk. Not only have you made a mistake and put yourself in danger, but now you're also compounding the error by putting your buddy at a significant risk.

So when you make a dive that might require staged decompression, talk it over with your buddy beforehand. You need to make very clear that each of you must work within your own limits. Of course, that means you each need to know what your limits are. If you're a beginner, approach those limits gingerly. Leave it to *Star Trek* to "Boldly go . . ." etc.

If you're working as a buddy team, stay within the limits of the less experienced partner. Peer pressure is tremendously powerful. In diving, in any risk sport, peer pressure can be deadly.

The very words I've heard people use to reassure less experienced divers are: "Don't worry, it's not that big a deal." Well, it is that big a deal.

So if I'm about to make a boat dive to look at a 110-foot wreck, I might start thinking, "You know, there's a good chance we're going to pick up some decompression penalty time on these dives." And I'll talk to my buddy and make plans accordingly.

If you're on a boat with a number of more experienced divers who are planning staged decompression dives, however, the peer pressure may make you think something like this: "They're going to be down there a long time; maybe I can work out a compromise. They're looking at 30 minutes of bottom time at 110 feet. Maybe my buddy and I can stay down for 20 minutes. That sounds good."

Actually, it sounds kind of dumb, doesn't it? But many divers say that's how they found themselves making their first staged decompression dives.

Another comment I've heard a lot: "I have a computer; it's going to give me the ceilings. It's going to say ascend to

60 feet, stay there a minute, ascend to 40 feet and stay there three minutes. If I run over a little on bottom time, my computer will figure everything out for me."

Your computer can't think for you any more than your buddy can.

If you spend enough time on boats, you're going to hear these and similar phrases. But you don't want to hear yourself saying them.

There are some steps you can take to protect yourself in case you find yourself in a staged decompression situation.

First, understand what staged decompression is. Don't blow from your maximum depth to your first stop. Ascend slowly to your first stop and stay there until your computer or your tables tell you it's time to move up. *Then* ascend to the next stop. That's the basics of it. You'll see quickly that it's not that complicated. However, failure to observe these simple rules can result in serious injury or death.

Second, understand staged decompression tables. These can be procured from various agencies; I like to get all my information from the same agency, because that way it's all based on the same algorithms, the same formulas. I don't want to mix and match. (In all probability, though, nothing bad is going to happen if you mix and match, as long as you always use the most conservative number.)

Sit down in your hotel room with your buddy and review your tables. Think about the possibilities. If you're going to have a bottom time of 20 minutes at 110 feet—this is within the no-decompression limits given on navy tables—ask yourselves, "What happens if we run 25 minutes? What happens if we run 30? Or 35?"

Go to your tables and look at each one of those situations and write down each of the requirements. If you stay there for 30 minutes, at what depth are you going to have to stop? And for how long are you going to have to be there?

The goal is: no surprises. You're starting to fill out the index card in your head that allows you to know what to do if you accidentally stay down longer than planned. And you have a written plan for various contingencies, which you're going to transfer to your underwater writing slate that you got in Open Water I to take down with you.

Third, keep this question in mind at all times: "Do I have enough air?" It's a good question. You've been taught to always return to the boat or shore with 500 pounds per square inch in your tank, so you've got a little reserve.

Divers, especially those who do open water diving for any length of time, tend to shave that just a little. I'm willing to bet that there're some of you out there who have arrived back at the boat just as you sucked the last bit of air from your tank. And what happened? What were the consequences?

None whatsoever. You got back on the boat, breathing. You blew through your reserves, no big deal. But think: What happens if you run out of air on your 20-foot stop? What happens if you've got to hang at stops for, say, 18 minutes at 20 feet, and 36 minutes at 10 feet, because for some perverse reason you decided to hang around at 110 feet for an hour? You get to 20, hang for a few minutes, and, whoops, you're out of air. Well, if you've got your buddy there and you're not endangering him, you could draw some of his air.

But, again, it's incorrect to put the other person at risk. If he has lots of air, and you have none, that's one situation. But generally, buddies use the same dive gear configuration. That means when you're both at the 20-foot stop, you're both running out of air.

So what're your options? That's right, you can't breathe water. You go up. What are the consequences in that situation?

DCS. You're very likely going to take a hit.

I know people who will argue with you all day long that they've blown to the surface after skipping a 10-foot stop and suffered nothing. Well, there are also people who have jumped in front of cars and not been hit. The likelihood, if you have to blow to the surface, is that you're going to get hit, and that's bad.

The bottom line is you don't want to be in a situation where you run out of air. And I say this as someone who has stupidly placed himself in that situation.

When you move on into technical diving, you'll discover that the whole question of gas management is at the center of all its challenges. Whether you're in an overhead environment, such as caves, or deep diving, or on a mixed-gas dive, gas management is at the heart of your planning. How much you have. How much you will use. How much you'll need to ascend. How much you hold into reserve. It's a very complicated subject. As you move into the technical dive arena, it's going to give you many, many headaches.

Gas Management

To understand and calculate how much air you'll need beneath the surface, it's important to know how much air you breathe above, a figure known as respiratory minute volume (RMV), a.k.a. surface consumption, which is defined as "the amount of air consumed in one minute on the surface."

That number varies by individual. And it changes as you become a more experienced diver.

When you began diving in Open Water I, you were probably really sucking that air. Your instructor told you, quite correctly, that as you became a better diver, the stress would lighten up a little and your breathing would shallow out.

The amount of air that you must take in is also genetically determined. For example, I'm a real sucker. I suck a lot less now than when I started diving years ago, but compared to some of my friends, I consume a fairly large amount of air.

Oddly, when calculating RMV, some people try to make the amount of air that they consume at the surface seem less than it really is by taking slow, deep breaths. What they want to show is that they are really calm in the water, well on their way to becoming experienced divers. What they need, however, is a real number. It's not a contest. You want a real number, because that number is how you calculate the amount of air you'll need at depth.

Your RMV also changes depending on exertion and health. If you have a head cold, you shouldn't be diving; still, if you just traveled halfway around the world and aren't going to let the sniffles keep you from the water, remember that your RMV will be greater than it would be in a normal situation. In cold water, too, your RMV is going to be greater: Your body's working harder to keep warm. Also, how hard are you going to be working? Will you be swimming a long distance? If you have to swim in and swim out, the heavy exertion will increase your RMV.

Your physical condition also affects your RMV. Are you in good shape? Bad shape? If you weigh 350 pounds and have trouble walking down a flight of steps, your RMV is going to be higher than it would be if you were in good cardiovascular health. These are all factors that charts and computers can't measure, and they all enter into the RMV equation.

So, let's assume you know from measuring your RMV that with your regular tank, an average aluminum 80-cubic-footer, you have 60 minutes of air. This means you can breathe it for 60 minutes on the surface. What happens when you descend? Your RMV changes with the depth. When the ambient pressure is doubled, the RMV doubles, too.

Thus, 60 minutes of air is only good for 30 minutes at 33 feet—two atmospheres; it's good for 20 minutes at 66 feet—three atmospheres. It's only good for 15 minutes at 99 feet. Remember the example of the 100-foot wreck dive? Fifteen minutes of bottom time at 100 feet cuts it too close. Even with no decompression stops at all, it will be impossible to complete that dive.

You have to factor in time from the surface to the bottom, bottom time, and ascent time. You might be able to scrape by if you take only 12 minutes of bottom time, and then make a safe ascent. But that, too, is cutting it really close.

So in this situation, what has your RMV number told you about a staged decompression? That you're in trouble. There isn't enough gas in the tank for you to stay down long enough to deal with the big decompression penalty you'll chalk up.

You now know that you can't make this dive safely. That's a pretty important piece of information. So, knowing this, what do you do?

Your first option is going to be a bigger mallet—a larger tank. In sport diving on the reefs, the small 80-foot tanks rule. But larger-capacity tanks are the norm everywhere else. For example, the popular Sherwood 120s, when fully inflated, hold half again as much air as an 80. That's the most basic way of changing your margins.

In order to get 60 minutes of breathing from an 80-cubic-foot tank, your RMV would have to be around 1⅓ cubic feet per minute. That same RMV using the larger tank will give you around 90 minutes of time. (Actually, the multiplier comes out to 90.22.)

A general rule, when calculating breathing gases, is to never round up. Always drop the numbers after the decimal point. Whether the number was 90.22 or 90.7, use 90. Why? Because even if you round up, the tank, in fact, will not contain 91 cubic feet of gas. It's much safer to round down, have a little extra margin of error there.

How does that 90 minutes translate as you go deeper? Well, at two atmospheres, 33 feet, you've got 45 minutes instead of 30. At 66 feet you've got the 30 minutes an 80-cubic-foot tank would allow. At 99 feet you've got about 22½ minutes—call it 22 minutes.

Now reexamine the dive to the 100-foot wreck. Say you want 15 minutes of bottom time at 100 feet. Do you have enough air with a 120-foot tank to do that under no-decompression limits? Yes, plus a little margin for safety.

What are some of your other options if there's a possibility that this may turn into a staged decompression dive? One is to go to doubles—that is, two separate tanks. Or you might want to carry a pony bottle. This is generally attached to your primary tank and maybe holds 40 cubic feet—half the size of a regular 80—with its own separate regulator. Either option will provide you with the extra air that you might need.

Alternatively, you might consider bringing a stage bottle—an extra single-scuba cylinder with a regulator—that would provide you with the emergency air that you might need in a staged ascent. You or your partner might carry the stage bottle down and tie it off where the anchor line is tied to the wreck, then retrieve the bottle and carry it up with you as you ascend.

Remember to plan the ascent so that if your dive requires a staged decompression, you're ready. You'll know where to stop and how long to hang there. Generally, you ascend the anchor line; if you're on a staged decompression dive, there may be a decompression line, which is a line dropped off the boat specifically to allow divers to do their decompression.

You can do a free-floating decompression, but if you're in the ocean, it's much easier to hang on a line. It's also much easier if you have a reference line. Attach yourself to the main line with a jon line—a 6-foot-long line with a hand loop and some kind of metal clip that can be attached to the anchor or decompression line. This way, you can concentrate on your buoyancy without worrying about the current or the surface conditions.

The first time I made a decompression dive, I hung on the anchor line with my hand—in a death grip, no less. I didn't have a jon line; I'd never even heard of one. There were heavy currents, so we had to hang on to the anchor line or we'd have been blown away. There were also 8- to 10-foot seas above us. As the boat went up, the line went up; as the boat came down, the line went down. It was a little bit like trying to do a decompression hang in a washing machine. I would not class it as great fun, and I would encourage you to have a jon line with you. It doesn't weigh anything, and can be stuck in a pocket.

Even if I'm using my computer, if I think there's a chance that I'm going to end up in a decompression situation, I have all my contingencies written on a slate that I have with me. If my computer dies, I can still complete my decompression using a watch and a submersible depth gauge.

Additionally, if I think a situation might turn into a decompression dive—in fact, on any dive deeper than 100 feet—I carry redundant equipment. Two computers, or one computer plus a depth gauge and a watch. I always carry a light, and if I think I'm going to *need* a light, I always carry two.

The key is to plan for your worst-case scenario. Prepare your alternative solutions. Know what you're going to do. Then you never have to worry about running out of air at 15 feet with three minutes left.

Everything I've discussed above falls into the category of dive planning. Every certification course teaches you to plan your dive—to get into the equipment, to talk to your buddy, to get the communications and gas-management issues resolved, to study the dive site, to plan the dive with your tables. Then, of course, you dive the plan.

Once you start planning your dives this way, you'll have a head start when you're ready to move into the next phase of diving. This is the way you'd plan a very deep dive, a wreck penetration dive, a cave dive. You'll find that, as you move up, planning becomes increasingly conservative.

At the very least, you should always have twice as much air as you think you might need. Once you move into penetration dives or deep dives, you use the "rule of thirds." That comes from cave diving and it means you use one-third of your air going in and one-third of your air coming out, with one-third held in reserve. In the worst case—say, at the farthest point of your dive your buddy has a catastrophic gas failure—there's enough gas for both of you to get out.

If I'm going deeper than 100 feet, or if there's any chance of penetrating a wreck, I shift in my own planning to the rule of thirds. IANTD recommends that any dive below 100 feet operate on this rule.

Here's a final suggestion: Before you actually attempt a staged decompression dive or accidentally find yourself on one, go to the next stage of training and take a deep air course.

These courses are offered by technical agencies such as the Professional Scuba Association, Technical Divers International (TDI—which, by the way, was founded by Bret Gilliam, co-author of a standard text on deep diving), and IANTD. The advantage of a deep air class is that you'll learn the right way—the safest way—to make a staged decompression dive, as opposed to the old hit-and-miss method.

11:
How
Deep
Is
Deep?

I keep coming back to deep diving because, unlike the case in some of the more esoteric forms of advanced diving, the dangers of deep diving are not obvious. It's unlikely (I hope) that a beginning diver will blindly enter a cave—the dangers are too clear. But going deep is another story.

Even if you head for the beginner-friendly Caribbean, the most beautiful dive trips are often along the various coral walls where it's very easy to drop past 100 feet, and even 130. The visibility is good, there's light, and the water's warm. However easy it seems, though, that doesn't negate the dangers and the increased risk factor that come with deep diving. A new-diver friend of mine (and editor of a magazine that includes stories about dive trips, so she should have known better) told me about a 160-foot dive on a wall in the Caribbean. Her rationale was that she had that legendary "gin-clear" visibility and there were lots of other divers around. She'd meant to go only to 100 feet, but the wall was so beautiful that she kept drifting downward. To her credit, when she realized she'd passed 160 feet, she didn't dawdle but immediately began a safe ascent.

In the last chapter, I described what you should be thinking about in case you find yourself in a staged decompression dive.

In this chapter, I'll do the same thing for deep dives. *The same warning applies: Do not make deep dives—below 100 feet— without specialized training!* At the very least, you need the deep diving classes offered by your certifying agency. And any diving beyond the 130-foot recreational limit requires specialized training that will be detailed later in this chapter.

Here are some things to think about, and some areas to focus on, *before* you're in a deep dive situation. A deep dive can still be a no-decompression-stop dive. However, as I discussed in the previous chapter, the deeper your dive is, the more likely it is that you'll have to do a staged decompression if something goes wrong and invalidates your primary dive plan.

One of the major complicating factors in deep diving is, strangely enough, ego. Once you have a firm grasp of the mechanics of diving, then its mental factors—the largest of which is ego—move into the forefront.

There are certain types of people who simply should never be involved in a deep dive. They present a risk to themselves, and to their partners.

And right now nearly all of you are thinking, "Well, I'm not one of those people. He must be talking about someone other than me."

That's your ego talking. It tells you, "I can do that. I can tough it out. I'm pretty sure I can get to that depth. I know I can make that work." All of which is pretty easy to say when you're on the surface in bright sunshine.

But before you let your ego do the talking, take a look at what deep dives commit you to.

As you descend deeper into the underwater environment, depending upon where you are, several things happen. First, it gets darker; the deeper you go, the less light there is. In some cases, like the northeastern United States or the Great Lakes, when you get down to 100 feet on a bad-visibility day, it's stone-cold dark. You've moved into a different realm. It's hard to explain just how dark it can be at 100 feet in lousy conditions, but even after a couple of night dives, a new diver might not be ready for it.

The fear of the dark is a very valid fear.

In addition, you've got increased pressure. And I'm not just speaking here of atmospheric pressure: there's a psychological pressure that comes with diving at depth. I certainly feel it; the people I dive with feel it. It's a sense of being—and I'm stealing this phrase from cave divers—away from the light. Sometimes cave divers who do deep penetration exploration dives will talk in terms of being "three, four hours from the light." And the deeper you go, the farther you move from it. I don't do deep dives every day of the week, but I have friends who come pretty close to that. And even after an enormous amount of time spent in the depths, they've never lost their respect, tinged with awe, for that deep landscape.

A second pressure that comes with depth is an awareness that there is no immediate access to the surface. At 30 feet, if something goes wrong, bam, inflate the vest, float to the surface, and you'll probably be safe. But divers know intellectually that if they blow to the surface from even 100 feet without regard for their ascent rate, they're potentially in a lot of trouble. Metaphorically, they're even farther away from the light.

In a real sense, the deeper you go, the more you enter into a "virtual" overhead environment, no different from being deep in a wreck or underwater cave. In a cave, you can look up and see the rock above you, and your mind clearly understands the situation. In the deeps, you can look up, and (visibility permitting, of course), why, there's the surface! Whenever I dive deep I always remind myself that, even if I can see the surface, there's an invisible "ceiling" between me and it. Despite what it looks like, I do not have immediate access to the surface—my ascent must be measured, or I will pay the consequences. The longer I stay at depth, the thicker that invisible ceiling becomes. It is as real as the corroded surface of a wreck, as unyielding as the unimaginable tons of rock forming the roof of a cave.

That mental pressure weighs on me and most of my friends. It's foolish to think it's not going to weigh on you, too. Especially on your first dives to depth. That psychic pressure, that knowledge of the invisible ceiling, is going to be there, right on top of you.

Another factor in deep diving is that all of a sudden you have to pay a lot more attention than you may be used to paying to your gear and gauges. You'll go through your air at a much faster rate at 100 feet than at the surface. If you're using up your air four times faster, you'll probably find yourself looking at your pressure gauge four times as often. And this chips away at you. Your focus is split. You're looking at the environment, which is scarier than a shallow-water environment; at the same time, you're having to pay more and more attention to your equipment. You also never forget that you have less margin for error here. You have to pay attention to your bottom time, you have to make sure you're back to the anchor rope, or the ascent line, on schedule. And you've got to pay attention to your buddy in less-than-optimum visibility. All that weighs on you.

These many stresses are a form of task loading. This is something every one of us has noticed at one time or another. Start with a really easy task; then pile task after task on top of it. Suddenly, the primary task gets harder. This is a critical point in diving, and in any risk sport.

The more complex the situation is, the more you have to do. The more you have to do perfectly, the more you come under the pressures of task loading. And the harder it is to perform the necessary tasks. Not everyone handles such stress well.

Bret Gilliam has described several different kinds of divers he doesn't think should progress into deeper training:

1. People *prone to panic*. Earlier in this book I mentioned the woman who thought she was drowning even though she was in a fully inflated BCD, was close to shore, and was surrounded by people. Panic can kill you. No, let me make that a little stronger—panic will kill you. It doesn't matter whether you're diving, mountain climbing, or skydiving. Panic is your single biggest enemy in high-stress situations.

   John Orlowski, in his great manual on cave diving, defines panic as "the ultimate in mental narrowing"— your mental capacity focuses to such an extent that all you can think of is the panic itself. Panic is the point at which there is no longer a relationship between what's happening to you and what you're doing about it.

   If you're prone to panic, you need to admit it to yourself. But that old devil ego makes it a hard thing to admit. Indiana Jones, after all, doesn't panic, even when he falls into a pit of snakes. However, it's better to admit to yourself that you're prone to panic while standing in your bedroom than it is to discover this fact at the bottom of a 120-foot dive with zero visibility. Because if you're not honest with yourself, you become a risk to yourself, your buddy, and the team.

   We all need to recognize ourselves as what we are, not as what we wish we were. We have to know where we're starting from before we can really go to the place we want to be.

   "Panic," writes Orlowski, "is the end of the line. It's usually both terminal and contagious. It's very hard to control, as far as any remedial actions are concerned."

2. Our old pal *James Bond*. This is someone who's trying very hard to prove something to himself. Unfortunately, you meet people like this in all risk sports. Bret Gilliam refers to them as having the "Top Gun syndrome." People who are trying to prove something to themselves invariably want to go beyond their capabilities, and they tend to create unrealistic short-term goals. But as Dirty Harry Callahan, in the movie *Magnum Force*, said, "A man's got to know his limitations."

Limitations are reality, not an issue of ego. When you're standing in your bedroom, think. What are your limitations? At what point are you out of your comfort zone? What are your capabilities?

I've met people who, after their fifth dive, have looked me in the eye and said, "I really would like to do a 200-foot dive, and I think I can pull it off in a month." Maybe they can, but I'm not going to be their partner on that dive. In fact, I wouldn't be their partner on a 130-foot dive.

3. Another personality to watch out for in other divers, and in yourself, is one that *plays along with peer pressure*. This includes the spousal pressure I discussed earlier. The wife says, "Honey, I know you've only done a 60-foot dive, but this is just a 90-footer. It's really not that much farther."

Yes, it is. But it's hard to look at your spouse, your buddy, or your friend and say, "No. That's not for me."

And why is this hard?

Because it chips away at your ego wall.

Somewhere beneath that "it's not really that much deeper" refrain is a little undercurrent, always unstated, but always implied, that says, "You know, if you were as good as I am, it wouldn't be a problem for you."

We've all experienced this from both ends. We've all put pressure on an individual to perform outside his or her capabilities. And we've all had pressure put on us to do the same.

It takes a strong ego to not only know what your limits are, but also stay within them.

There's an interesting subculture within cave diving that demonstrates an important ethic. Within that specialized fraternity (or sorority, as the case may be), it's considered acceptable to "call" (abort) a dive for any reason. It doesn't matter if you're starting the dive, finishing it, or in the middle. It doesn't matter if you've traveled around the world for the dive. If one member of the party calls the dive, the dive is over.

That part's pretty normal in dive circles. The unique thing within the cave community is that it is considered very bad etiquette—in fact, it's considered offensive—to ask that person why he or she called the dive. It's just not done.

I've seen a cave dive called by one of the top cave divers in the world. He drove to a site in north Florida, an area where years before he had helped lay the guidelines to map the caves. For him, it was the equivalent of a dive in the backyard swimming pool. But he got out of his pickup truck, took one look around, and announced to his diving partner, "We're going to a bar to get a beer. We're not going in the water today." And they headed off to the bar.

His partner didn't ask why the dive was called. He wouldn't even have thought of asking.

I've been on dives that have been called for reasons I couldn't fathom on my own. I have called dives for reasons that, if you were to ask, I could only describe as "bad karma."

But once you move into risk realms, outside of your own comfort zone, ambiguous feelings of doubt are as real and as valid as those reasons we can more readily accept. A "bad feeling" about a dive is every bit as valid a reason for calling a dive as a regulator that refuses to work properly.

Any reason is an acceptable reason.

One of the points that John Orlowski makes over and over is that it takes a very secure ego to be able to say, "I'm not going to do this, and I'm not going to explain it, either."

That strength is something to work toward.

Just as important is arriving at a point where, if your dive buddy, spouse, or friend says, "I'm really uncomfortable with this," then you can automatically say, "We're not doing it. We're not going to do it because you're uncomfortable with it."

12:
Rapture
of the
Deep
and
Other
Myths

As you dive deeper and deeper, the narcotic effects of nitrogen become more pronounced. It's what used to be called the "rapture of the deep," and people who watch old dive movies will automatically assume that this rapture is going to happen to them.

I remember telling my parents I was going on one of my first deep dives. They said, "What are you going to do about rapture of the deep?"

Nitrogen narcosis affects every diver to one degree or another. If you go down below a certain depth, usually around 90 feet, you'll experience narcosis. As seems the case with much of diving physiology, the exact mechanism of this effect isn't totally understood. Symptoms, though, can include euphoria (that pesky rapture), drowsiness, a false sense of security and unconcern for safety, a loss of fine motor coordination, and a general impairment of analytic abilities—at the very moment when you need to be very clear-headed.

In my case, it's not so much rapture of the deep as it is nausea of the deep. I don't feel a pronounced narcosis until I get below the recreational depths, and when I do, it's almost always preceded by a wave of nausea. Then, at a certain depth, I feel as if my thoughts are crawling slowly from one side of my head to the other. If I go 10 feet up—or, strangely enough, 10 feet down—the symptoms abate.

Narcosis varies from individual to individual, even day to day, and there are many predisposing factors. For example, a common occurrence in the Caribbean is divers with terrible hangovers discovering that they're terribly narked at depth. But lots of factors, including fatigue and even fear, can affect narcosis. That's important to know, since on some of your first deep dives you're going to have some fear.

The harder you work, the more you elevate levels of

fatigue poisons such as carbon dioxide in your bloodstream, and the more likely you are to get narked.

There's a two-pronged attack you should make on narcosis. First comes your own mindset. Divers have said to me, "Oh my God, I hope I don't get really narked on this dive." Well, that doesn't reflect the reality of diving. You are going to get narked; it's a physical process.

The better attitude is, "I'm going to get narked and I want to be aware of it. I want to monitor myself for signs of it, but it's going to happen, and it's no big deal."

Because the physical process of becoming narked can be affected by how you respond to it, it's important that you constantly monitor yourself. Some people are good at acknowledging they're narked; they understand that they've suffered a degradation of their faculties. Some people never have a clue.

The key thing is go into the dive acknowledging that you're going to be narked and remaining watchful for the symptoms. If you detect a fogging of your mental processes, trouble reading your gauges, or an odd feeling of well-being, stop. If you're on a descent, stop and focus very clearly on something. I usually focus on the descent line, or, if I'm close to a wall, the rock and coral itself. If I'm in open water, I sometimes focus on my instrumentation or come to a complete stop and focus on maintaining neutral buoyancy.

In short, I get a grip, then continue my descent. *Pause, get a grip, then continue.* If you're having trouble getting that grip, ascend a few feet and wait. Remember, you're not in a race to get to the bottom, especially not on your first deeper dives.

When I'm diving at depth, I'm constantly asking myself questions. *Am I narked? Can I detect any degradation in my fac-*

ulties? Do I feel light-headed? Do I feel a drunkenness, a sense of euphoria? Am I having problems reading my instrumentation? When my buddy asks me a question, am I having trouble responding?

The second prong of dealing with narcosis has to do with your buddy. Your buddy should be watching you for signs, just as you're watching your buddy for them. Ideally, when you make your deep dives in your advanced open water class, your instructor watched for narcosis signs with you and was able to show you at what point you were narked, and how you responded.

I like to "talk" to my buddy on a deep descent, exchanging hand signals. It's my way of monitoring him, and his way of monitoring me.

It's been my experience that if I'm looking for it, narcosis is not that big a deal. It's when I'm denying it that it really whacks me.

Assume you're going to be narked, and create mental index cards for it.

Also, discuss it with your buddy before the dive. Talk about the level at which you get narked. Talk about the symptoms that you've experienced. Tell your buddy what to look for in you.

I dove with one buddy whose endless way of checking to see if we were narked at depth was to add 2 + 2 and see if we got 4. On your next deep dive, takes some notes on your slate while you're on the bottom. Compare this with your normal handwriting. At a couple of hundred feet on air, my notes to myself appear to be in Sanskrit.

You're not going to be at tip-top mental sharpness at depth. And that means you've got to make your dive profile as simple as possible. On your first deep dives, don't try out a dive plan that you haven't used before.

As for physical preparations, make sure all equipment is in tip-top shape. And the first piece of equipment that you want to make sure is in excellent working order is yourself.

No drinking before diving. Also, don't tie one on the night before, because a hangover is just as dangerous as a drink. In my own case, I err on the side of moderation before a deep dive. I might have a beer with dinner the night before, but that's it. If it's a dive that's new to me, or particularly taxing, I'll completely abstain the day before.

No drugs—nonprescription, prescription, or recreational. Consult your doctor if you're on prescribed medication. I avoid even decongestants on deeper dives. On a 60-foot dive, I might use a decongestant beforehand to clear my head and make it easier for me to clear my ears. On a 130-foot dive, no way.

Eat well. I eat a good breakfast, but avoid grease because I'm occasionally prone to seasickness. If I'm going to be sloshing around on a boat, toast and peanut butter is about as risky as I'm willing to go. This is important because on a deep dive, I'm not going to be taking antiseasickness medication.

Be well rested. If I've got a rough series of dives to below 100 feet ahead, I know I'm going to need all my strength.

As to the gear itself, always use your own equipment on deep dives. If I'm traveling long distances to make shallow reef dives—60 feet or less—I tend to rent equipment. If I know I'll be making deep dives, though, I always use my own equipment.

Don't try anything new on your first deep dive. You have enough task loading to worry about without also trying to read a new computer, test a new wet suit, or acclimatize to a dry suit. You want 100 percent reliable equipment that you're familiar and comfortable with.

At the point when you start making deep dives, think about getting rid of the danglies. This is all that equipment that's hanging off you. Go dive the shallow reefs off Key West and you'll see divers with so much stuff hanging off them that they look like that creature in *Aliens*. But anything hanging down can get hung up somewhere, and anything that gets hung up somewhere can cause you problems.

As you move into deeper diving, think in terms of streamlining. For example, settle on a position for your spare regulator, your octopus, your alternative air source. You want an item of gear to be in the same place whenever you reach for it. And you should set up a tethering system to make sure it stays there.

There are as many different ways to rig equipment as there are divers. The main thing is to settle on a system that works for you, then stick with it. You should practice using your system, too. Practice finding and grabbing your octopus without flailing around.

Tether your instrument console to your vest. I use a short piece of bungee cord, so even though the console is out of the way, if I want to look at it I need only pull on its tether. A piece of surgical tubing works as well.

To determine the placement of equipment, talk to more experienced divers. Ask them the pros and cons of their gear arrangements.

Take, for example, your knife, a tool that you'll use to extract yourself from anything you might get tangled in. Most divers strap their knifes to the inside of the calf muscle, usually on their weak leg. But can you envision a situation in which you've become tangled in such a way that you cannot get to the knife? When you start making penetration dives into wrecks, you'll know what I mean. You should consider carefully where you carry your knife, and even carry a second, smaller one.

I carry my main knife zip-tied to the low-pressure inflator on my BCD or wings, so I know where it is all the time—within a hand's reach. I carry a backup small knife in my pocket with my backup small light. This is the time to think about not just streamlining, but also redundancy.

Above 100 feet it's safe to assume that your buddy's gear will serve as the redundancy. But below 100 feet, it's very important for you to have all that redundant gear I discussed earlier.

Choose an exposure suit suitable to the temperatures you're going into. One of the most common problems I see among divers is getting cold because they've chosen the wrong type of exposure suit: too thin a wet suit, or a wet suit when a dry suit was needed. Hypothermia (insufficient body heat) is a constant problem when you're immersed in water that is at less than your body temperature. The drop in your core temperature causes a corresponding drop in your mental processes. You'll become uncoordinated, drowsy, and, eventually, unconscious and dead.

Remember, water doesn't have to be freezing cold to be dangerous. And it doesn't take that much exposure. Recently, for a television news show, I agreed to make a couple of river-surfing runs (sort of like white-water rafting without the raft) on a local river. The water was cold, but the runs were short to accommodate the cameras, and it was a blisteringly hot day. I figured I'd be in the water less than five minutes per run, and in a full wet suit, booties, and gloves. By the end of the second run, though, I was so hypothermic that I blew my entry into the last small waterfall and had to be plucked out of the water downstream by my safety kayaker. It took several minutes in the sun before

143

I was coordinated enough to take off my gear. Oh well, it looked better on video.

Know your dive site; know what the temperature is likely to be, and also what the worst-case temperature is for that time of year at that depth. Then plan for that worst case.

Occasionally, I have had to shuck parts of my wet suit, such as my jacket, for the next dive, but generally, I've been very happy that I was warm. I can recall times when I took some ribbing on a boat for being overdressed; after the first dive, I didn't get any ribbing anymore. Instead, people wanted to know if I had any extra gear.

Make sure that the boat you're going out on has a full set of rescue equipment, including an oxygen kit. This is something that shouldn't have to be mentioned—every boat should have an oxygen kit. Unfortunately, not all do. If you're going out with a large group, make sure you ask about this, and make sure you know where that oxygen is. I asked the question once and the boat's captain showed me the oxygen tank. But I looked at the gauge, and it read EMPTY. When I pointed this out to the captain, he responded, "You know, oxygen costs a lot."

Any boat that you're out on should have complete rescue, first-aid, and oxygen gear available to you.

13:
The
Next
Steps:
Technical
Diving

Y ou've been diving for a year or so. You've gone through your advanced open water training, you've got a year's worth of dives in. You're sticking with it, because, from the very beginning, you had a plan—your diving goals.

Now it's time for what I like to think of as a midcourse correction. Ask yourself whether diving is yielding the kind of results that you anticipated. Are you getting what you expected from scuba diving?

I like to debrief people who drop out of diving after one or two years, or, in some cases, three to five years. I ask them what series of events made them decide to give up something that had taken such a large investment of time and money. The answer that often comes up is "I wasn't getting out what I was putting in."

When I pursue the question, the answers tend to reflect the notion that the entire universe of diving is shallow reef diving, as if all of the sport could be contained in the Caribbean destination dive resorts.

I also find that most people who drop out of the sport had not given a lot of thought to goal setting early on. And that the ones who did failed to stop after a year or so to evaluate their situation.

So this is a good time to stop and question yourself. Do you feel you're on your way to achieving your goals? Are those goals still valid?

It's worth sitting down, taking out a piece of paper, and dividing it down the middle. On one half of the paper, list what you really like about diving. On the other, list what you really *don't* like. Take a look at the list—item by item, on each side of the paper.

What is it that you like? *I really love the travel. I really love going to a foreign country. I really love meeting people in a foreign country, and, oh yeah, diving in a foreign country.*

Then go over to the other side and see what you really don't like about diving. Is it the crowds? The expense? Is it that you're uncomfortable diving on your own? Are you uncomfortable pushing to the limits of your ability?

Break it down, and then break it down even farther. Go to the next level: *I really hate cattle boats. I really hate groups of 10 to 12 people all looking at one poor terrified moray eel. I feel like a complete idiot, I've spent a lot of money. I don't like the divemasters in the Caribbean.*

It's fun to make a list with someone you dive with, so that you can bounce ideas off each other and evaluate entries on both sides. This also keeps you honest: You say, "I like those deep dives. I like to get way down there when things get really scary. I've enjoyed that." And your buddy points out that you called your last three dives halfway through because you were rattled.

With some real information about what you like and dislike, go back now to your original goals. Ask yourself if they're still valid. If they are, all the better. Because you're now ready to move onto the next stage of accomplishing them.

If your goals aren't still valid, why not? Did you discover that when you started diving, things you thought you'd like didn't turn out to be so great? Is it that the goal is still too far away? Or was the goal too small to keep you interested?

This questioning process is geared to help keep you from dropping out of scuba. It's also a process that I've used successfully in a number of other risk sports. When I started moving into sports' more extreme edge, I wanted a consistent method for becoming involved in often complicated, often dangerous activities. How do I plan? What sort of training should I get? How do I set my goals? What do I need to do for training? What do I need to buy? My self-questioning led me to the process I've outlined for you here.

The reevaluation step is every bit as important as the first goal-setting step.

And now, where do you go from here?

More and more divers are looking for what's beyond the limits of recreational diving. If you're one, you may be wondering what you can do to further your skills as a diver, to push yourself a little harder, to take yourself into realms where the majority of people are not able or willing to go.

You can find the answer to "What next" at any of a number of technical dive training agencies. A few years back, there were virtually none of these. But now you have a choice—in almost every area of the country, you can get technical instruction.

Technical Diving

Technical diving is diving that takes place outside the realms of traditional scuba.

That can mean deeper than the 130-foot recreational "limit." It can mean diving in overhead environments such as caverns and caves, or penetrating deep into wrecks. It can mean breathing mixes other than the air—79 percent nitrogen, 21 percent oxygen. It can mean a combination of any of these.

Technical diving presents a greater risk than recreational diving. It pushes limits, and, consequently, the subjective and objective risks increase.

Technical dive training is expensive. It's far more expensive than recreational. Why should that be? As I discussed in chapter 6, recreational scuba training tends to be undervalued; there are a lot of instructors, which translates into a lot of discounting. Once you move into the technical regions, you're going to have to pay what the instruction is worth.

Technical training is a major commitment of time; a major financial commitment; and a mental commitment, because you're going to work harder for your technical training than you did for that first C-card.

I would argue that it's very much worth it.

Technical training goes beyond advanced recreational scuba training. Think of it as the logical extension of the specialty recreational training you've already had. Right now, though, the technical arena has yet to fully organize itself into a specific course sequence the way recreational scuba has. Rather, it's more of a restaurant menu, with lots of options. It's up to you to sort out the difference between appetizers and entrées.

Let me make a couple of suggestions as to the best way to approach continued education in technical diving. The first class for a recreational diver who is interested in getting into technical diving, has at least 100 dives under his or her belt, and is comfortable on the fringes of recreational diving, is a deep air class.

Deep Air

What will you learn in a deep air class?

You'll learn about diving safely below the 130-foot limit of recreational diving. You'll learn more about the effects of narcosis and more about staged decompression. You'll learn more about the way you may respond physically and psychologically at increasing depth levels.

The deep air instruction course taught by Hal Watts at 40 Fathoms Grotto in central Florida is one of my all-time favorite dive courses. Hal's team of instructors takes you from 100 feet to 240 feet on air, in stages. For each stage, there's classroom instruction, dive planning instruction, and the supervised dives themselves.

Be aware that many excellent dive instructors consider 200 feet to be the maximum for air. If you consider it carefully and choose to go on, this is a good place to do so. Hal Watts probably knows more about diving deep on air than any man alive.

Starting at the 100-foot level helps rid you of bad habits that you may have picked up so far. The instructors can ferret out what you've been doing wrong, and then work with you—first tell you the right way, then show you the right way, then help you ingrain the right way into your own diving. When you make the two required dives, they'll watch you very closely to make sure that you're doing each one safely. Compare this to the usual way people go deeper: "Well, I'm doing okay at 130; I'll go ahead and do a dive on my own to 150 feet and see how I feel. Then maybe I'll drop down to 180. That should be a lot of fun."

The obvious advantages of doing your deep air dives within a controlled situation are safety and knowing what to expect at each level. If you're interested in the deeps, you absolutely should take a course, with supervised dives, before descending on your own. It is much safer for you to find out how you're going to respond to depth while there are trained safety divers with you and you know what to expect.

For example, on my 240-foot air dive, Hal Watts himself was the safety diver, along with two instructors. You could not ask for a better, more skilled, more competent diver to be with as you work through that kind of depth.

Such dives are also tremendous confidence builders. As I discussed in the last chapter, on narcosis, you have to find out how your body responds to nitrogen at each different level. One of the most powerful things you can do to keep from being disabled by narcosis is anticipate how it will feel and mentally prepare for it. A course is a way, in a controlled situation, for you to fill out that particular mental index card.

For example, I learned that my response to narcosis at 170 feet is totally different than at 180 feet, which is in turn totally different than at 200 feet. I found that I pass through a zone of very bad narcosis—waves of nausea, the whirlies, everything spinning around my head—at about 185 feet—and then it clears up. (But, remember, everyone is different.) Believe me, this knowledge alone is worth the cost of the training course.

Armed with this knowledge, I know what's coming. And knowing what's coming ameliorates it tremendously.

You'll also learn other good strategies for dealing with narcosis in a course, including focusing and mental imaging: *Yes, I know I'm going to be narked. I'm going to monitor that. My buddy's going to monitor that. We're going to be constantly monitoring each other.*

A deep air course:

° Gives you an objective way of knowing how your body is going to respond to depth.
° Allows you to get that information within a safe, controlled situation.

° Allows you to study the theory of deep air diving in the classroom at the same time you're making dives in practice.

° Builds your confidence—it's the single largest confidence builder for you as a diver.

I unconditionally recommend that your first step outside recreational diving be to take a course in deep air.

Technical Nitrox

What comes after deep air? The logical next step—and it goes hand in hand with deep air diving—is what's called a Technical Nitrox course. Nitrox is air enriched with additional oxygen, and it has become extremely common recreationally.

Nitrox allows more bottom time, but the price you pay is strict depth restrictions. At 60 feet, for instance, the bottom time on air is 55 minutes. On nitrox, it's 100 minutes. Depending on which "mix" of nitrox you're breathing (32 percent oxygen and 36 percent oxygen are the most common, as opposed to normal air at 21 percent oxygen), you may be required to restrict your depths to 100 feet (36%) or 130 feet (32%). Unlike the 130-foot floor for recreational diving, there is nothing arbitrary about the nitrox restrictions. Oxygen, so necessary to our survival, becomes toxic at depth, based on complicated laws of partial pressure and oxygen exposure. *Nitrox operating limits must be strictly adhered to!* Unfortunately, many divers don't understand the difference between personal limits and those limits set by physics and gas theory. If you have any problems in that area at all, I suggest you stick with air.

That said, I always use nitrox when it's available and appropriate for the depth involved. I'm not so much interested in the added bottom time as I am in the added safety factor. I might use nitrox, for example, with my air-based computers, which gives me about a 20 percent safety factor. Also, I have found that the added oxygen content of nitrox leaves me less fatigued after a day of diving than air does. Most divers I know who use nitrox regularly report the same lessened fatigue, although a minority feel no difference.

This really hit home after a day of cave diving, which included five shallow dives into different cave systems. We used a custom blend of nitrox with a relatively high oxygen content and figured all out bottom times for air. Even after five dives and lugging cave gear around, I felt pretty good at the end of the day. Had I been on air, I would have been whipped. Remember, fatigue is a risk factor.

In a Technical Nitrox class you'll work more on learning the ins and outs of staged decompression. You'll learn that you can shorten decompression stops or make them safer by varying the breathing mix that you use at various depths.

It's also a math-heavy class. I found it mentally exhausting, but it's necessary if you plan to go on. Or if you hope to someday use trimix—another deep breathing mix. And you need a Technical Nitrox class before you can step up and take advantage of some of the computerized decompression planning programs that are available now for the personal computer.

A word of warning:

Just because you can buy a decompression program that allows you to compute for gases at different levels, and you can then go home and mix those gases in your garage, it doesn't mean you know what you're doing. It is critical that you take a Technical Nitrox course before you try anything of the sort.

I know divers who have never had Technical Nitrox training, but who routinely use enriched air for staged decompression. I've also seen them make mistakes, and sooner or later, some of them are going to pay. The class is cheap insurance. When you look at the whole range of technical diving, deep air and Technical Nitrox are the two fundamental classes that you must have before you move into the more specialized classes.

Cave Diving

Cave diving is the type that I enjoy the most, that I try to do the most, and that represents my own goals in diving.

Generally, cave diving instruction is divided into three sessions: cavern diving, single-tank cave diving, and full cave.

Cavern diving is also seen as specialty by some dive organizations—a cavern being defined as a space in which you have constant direct access to the surface. You've not penetrated to the point that you can no longer see the light, or that you no longer have direct access to the light.

I suggest taking even cavern instruction from one of the technical agencies, if possible. Why does this require special instruction? People die in caverns every year. The sun goes down, the sun goes behind a cloud, a thunderstorm comes up, and divers can't find their way out of a cavern, even if there's clear, unobstructed access to the surface.

The first level of cavern instruction is fundamental to understanding what's to follow. It gives you a little background on caves and caverns themselves—an understanding of this particular underwater environment. What comes next is the entire cave diving instruction sequence. This sequence tends to take more than a week, which is why it is usually broken down into the three segments. It's very, very stressful. I would class this as one of the most demanding instruction sequences I've ever gone through. It's also very precise, and there's a tremendous amount of diving involved. During the entire course, your instructor is watching you and evaluating you to see if you really belong in an overhead environment.

I was one of two students in my cave class. I passed, the other student didn't. The other student was also an open water instructor with ten years' experience. Caves will test every single thing you've ever learned in any other form of diving. Diving them will take all your skills and previous training. However, if you're willing to make this commitment, I think there is no better way of becoming a master scuba diver than to go through full cave training.

In an overhead environment, *there's no margin for error.* But for me, the rewards of that environment are huge. It is as close as you can get to outer space while still on this planet.

A lot of people my age had great fantasies of becoming astronauts, and unfortunately, that just didn't happen for all of us. The space program wound down; plus, for those of us with bad eyesight, those of us without engineering degrees, those of us who weren't test pilots, space remained out of reach.

But if you're willing to make the commitment, you can go to inner space.

Trimix

For those people who are drawn to the deeps the next stage—or an alternative to the cave stage—is trimix. Trimix is a mixture of nitrogen, oxygen, and helium, with the helium offsetting a portion of the nitrogen and oxygen. Breathing less nitrogen means its effects on you are also reduced, and this allows you to "choose" the *equivalent depth* that you want.

That means you can dive to 300 feet, but by adjusting the mix, you'll have the narcotic *effects* of nitrogen at 125 feet. This allows you to work with a clear head; thus, trimix is a much safer way of making deep dives. Most technical divers in this country won't go below 150 to 200 feet unless they have mixes.

Trimix is another math-heavy class. You'll spend a huge amount of time in a classroom learning about gases, the mixing of gases, and the physiology of breathing. You're also going to learn the ins and outs of oxygen toxicity—yes, our pal oxygen can kill us, if we're not very careful.

It's complicated. Oxygen becomes toxic when a partial pressure of greater than one atmosphere is breathed for a period of time. As we dive deeper, however, there's an increase in the partial pressure of oxygen, which we must take into account as we plan our dives.

Still, though, if you're fascinated by deep diving, and you're really fascinated by deep wrecks, then you'll need trimix instruction. Yes, it's expensive and time-consuming. And once you finish the instruction, you'll discover that mix diving costs a lot more than recreational scuba. Mix can cost anywhere from $50 to $70 per tank, as opposed to a $5 fillup of compressed air.

So, there's a tradeoff for everything.

Other Specialties

I shudder to make any recommendations on rebreather technology because it's changing so fast. But I suspect that sometime in the next five or six years, as the price comes down, rebreathers—those military-derived devices that allow you to recirculate a portion of the air you're breathing—are probably going to become the norm for recreational diving.

Unfortunately, lacking a crystal ball, I can't tell you that for sure. The trend certainly seems to be going that way. But rebreather technology is growing so rapidly that anything I tell you now may no longer be true in the near future.

I purposely have not discussed divemaster or instructor training. In the past, divers interested in refining their skills have looked to the demanding divemaster/instructor ratings courses. I feel that, given the present quality and availability of technical training, there's no reason to go through these sequences. You'll better advance your diving on the technical instruction route.

157

For your technical dive training, think in terms of overlap. For instance, if you're fascinated by diving wrecks recreationally, say 100- to 130-foot wrecks, but also want to go inside them on a penetration dive, I unconditionally recommend taking cavern and single-tank cave courses. Why? Because the overhead environment is not only found in caves; it can also be present in wrecks. The strategies that cave divers teach can thus help keep you alive in wreck diving.

By the way, if you're looking at deep wreck diving, another option is a deep wreck diving course. The technical certifying agency lists don't usually list such courses by name. However, if you talk to the instructors, they may be able to structure a course to your needs. I'm sure they'll tell you to take at least a basic cave course, which teaches you how to deal with the overhead environment. And they'll couple that with offering you some strategies specific to wrecks.

But the main thing is to never stop learning. I think that when people lose interest in learning more about diving, they start drifting away from the sport.

As you've seen throughout this book, I'm a staunch proponent of instruction. Instruction is cheap compared to hospital time. And with all risk sports, the very best instruction you can afford is only barely good enough.

Can you teach yourself to go beyond the range of technical scuba safely? Maybe. But that's a big maybe. The consequences of screwing up far outweigh the cost of getting instruction. Especially given the high quality of instruction that is now available.

Check the end of this book for a list of technical dive agencies and what they offer. Give them a call.

Resources

Certifying Agencies

ANDI (American Nitrox Divers International)
74 Woodcleft Avenue
Freeport, NY 11520
(516) 546-2026
Fax (516) 546-6010

IANTD (International Association of Nitrox & Technical Divers)
9628 NE 2nd Avenue, Suite D
Miami Shores, FL 33138-2767
(305) 751-4873
Fax (305) 751-3958

NAUI (National Association of Underwater Instructors)
P.O. Box 4650
Montclair, CA 91763-1150
(800) 553-NAUI
(714) 621-5801
Fax (714) 621-6405

PADI (Professional Association of Dive Instructors)
1251 East Dyer Road, Suite 100
Santa Ana, CA 92705-5605
(800) 729-7234
(714) 540-7234
Fax (714) 540-2609

PSA (Professional Scuba Association)
9487 NW 115th Avenue
Ocala, FL 34482-1007
(904) 368-7974
Fax (904) 351-1924

SSI (Scuba Schools International)
2619 Canton Court
Ft. Collins, CO 80525-4498
(800) 821-4319
(303) 482-0883
Fax (303) 482-6157

Instructors Mentioned in This Book

David Feeney
Scuba Network Brooklyn
290 Atlantic Avenue
Brooklyn, NY 11201
(718) 802-0700

John and Shelley Orlowski
Aquaspeleo
Route 5, Box 128E
Live Oak, FL 32060
(904) 776-1191

Wings Stock
Ocean Odyssey Dive Center
860 17th Avenue
Santa Cruz, CA 95062
(408) 475-3483

Hal Watts
Forty Fathom Grotto
9487 NW 115th Avenue
Ocala, FL 34482-1007
(904) 368-7974

Dive Publications

Aqua
3886 State Street
Santa Barbara, CA 93105
(805) 682-7177

Dive Travel
500 Seabright Avenue
Santa Cruz, CA 95062
(408) 459-6188

Rodale's Scuba Diving
6600 Abercorn Street
Savannah, GA 31405
(912) 351-0855

Skin Diver
6420 Wilshire Boulevard
Los Angeles, CA 90048
(213) 782-2000

Sport Diver
330 West Carlton Avenue
Winter Park, FL 32789
(407) 628-4802